"Charles Hodges carefully and methodically helps us understand how our culture has come to view depression through the lens of disease. After unpacking this view, Charlie shows how God provides a genuine hope that can't be found in our culture's treatment of depression. Read this book and begin to view depression and sadness through a different lens. You'll be glad you did."

—**Dr. Amy Baker**, Director of Ministry Resources, Counselor, Instructor, Faith Ministries, Lafayette, IN

"Finally a book that cuts through the fog and confusion of moods, medications and the Bible without being overly technical and critical! I can think of no one better suited to write this than Charlie. His use of Scripture secures the truth in God's unchanging Word, and he writes with the compassion and warmth of an experienced physician and counselor. The Christian community owes him a debt of gratitude for giving us such a helpful resource."

—**Brad Bigney**, Senior Pastor and Biblical Counselor, Grace Fellowship Church, Florence, KY

"Dr. Hodges' conversational style and winsome presentation of key biblical and physical issues provides good advice regarding sadness, depression and bipolar diagnoses from a balanced perspective of a gracious physician and a wise biblical counselor. This resource is a must-read for pastors, counselors and ministry leaders, and for anyone who struggles in these areas."

—**Kevin Carson**, Biblical Counseling Department Chair, Baptist Bible College and Theological Seminary, Springfield, MO

"Dr. Hodges's book is an important contribution to the biblical counseling literature regarding depression and bipolar disorder. He provides a robust treatment plan for sadness through a loving relationship with Christ and a growing understanding of his word. Biblical counselors will benefit from the historical elements and the biblical solutions for those who experience sadness due to the weight of living in a sin-cursed world."

—**Dr. Rob Green**, Pastor of Counseling and Seminary Ministries, Faith Church, Lafayette, IN.

"The biblical counseling movement is blessed to have godly physicians like Charles Hodges who are both skilled scientists and committed theologians. You will be helped by Dr. Hodges' careful and copious research on contemporary ideas about mood disorders. You will also receive practical truth on how to help those the Lord brings to you who are struggling with sadness and despair."

—**Dr. Steve Viars**, Senior Pastor, Faith Church, Lafayette, IN

"Charles Hodges gave himself a big assignment: To explain how society's views of sadness and depression have changed so that they are seen almost completely as medical problems experienced by rapidly growing numbers of people. He documents how an increased reliance on medication has not eased people's pain but complicated it. In this fascinating book, Hodges summarizes scientific research in a way that allows readers to make up their own minds, and he illustrates how biblical counseling leads sufferers to the answers they seek. He demonstrates confidence in Scripture, respect for sound medical practice, and compassion and hope for his patients and counseling clients. This book is worth reading."

—**Susan Lutz**, Biblical Counselor, pastor's wife, editor

"*Good Mood, Bad Mood* is an exceptionally clear and hopeful book explaining what the diagnosis of bipolar means and what it does not mean. The book contains biblical illustrations, patient illustrations, and personal illustrations from Dr. Hodges' life and medical practice. It is an engaging, well-thought-out, and compelling read. This will help anyone who struggles with depression to carefully assess what is really happening and, as a consequence, turn to the Lord. I will definitely use *Good Mood, Bad Mood* in my counseling ministry."

—**Martha Peace**, Author and Biblical Counselor

"*Good Mood, Bad Mood* will be good news for thousands of discouraged Christians. Written by a compassionate physician who thinks outside of the medical box but within the parameters of Scripture, this eye-opening book addresses a problem for which the medical profession has limited answers. I highly recommend it to all who have questions about the true nature of their "mood" disorders."

—**Lou Priolo**, Director of Biblical Counseling, Eastwood Presbyterian Church, Montgomery, AL and author

GOOD MOOD, BAD MOOD

HELP AND HOPE FOR DEPRESSION AND BIPOLAR DISORDER

CHARLES D. HODGES, M.D.

Shepherd Press
Wapwallopen, Pennsylvania

Good Mood, Bad Mood
© 2012 by Charles D. Hodges Jr., M.D.
Trade Paperback ISBN: 978-1-936908-509

eBook ISBN
Mobi format: ISBN 978-1-936908-516
ePub format: ISBN 978-1-936908-523

Published by Shepherd Press
P.O. Box 24, Wapwallopen, Pennsylvania 18660

Scripture taken from *The New American Standard Bible,* © Copyright 1960, 1962, 1963, 1968, 1971, 1972, 1973, 1975, 1977, 1995 by the Lockerman Foundation. Used by Permission. Italics or bold text within Scripture quotations indicate emphasis added by author.

Page design and typesetting by Lakeside Design Plus
Cover design by Tobias' Outerwear for Books
First Printing, 2012
Printed in the United States of America

VP 25 24 23 22 21 20 19 18 17 16 15 14 13
14 13 12 11 10 9 8 7 6 5 4 3 2 1

Library of Congress Cataloging-in-Publication Data
Hodges, Charles D., Jr.
 Good mood, bad mood : help and hope for depression and bipolar disorder /
by Charles D. Hodges Jr., M.D.
    pages cm
 Includes bibliographical references.
 ISBN 978-1-936908-50-9 (print book : alk. paper) -- ISBN 978-1-936908-52-3
(epub edition) -- ISBN 978-1-936908-51-6 (kindle edition) 1. Depression,
Mental. 2. Depression, Mental--Religious aspects--Christianity. 3.
Manic-depressive illness--Religious aspects--Christianity. I. Title.
RC537.H625 2012
616.85'27--dc23
                                2012044019

eBook: *Good Mood, Bad Mood*

Go to: http://www.shepherdpress.com/ebooks

Contents

To Helen,
my dear wife and best friend for forty-three years,
who always thought I would write a book someday.
Thank you for patiently giving me the time to write
and encouraging me to stick with it.

Acknowledgments

There are many people I want to thank for their part in this book. To the good people at Shepherd Press and to Rick and Bonnie Irvin, thank you for reading my earliest manuscript and seeing the opportunity in it.

I am deeply indebted to Jay Younts, who read the third rewrite chapter by chapter, as I wrote it mostly new again. Thank you so very much for your patience and guidance. I enjoyed the fellowship. Sue Lutz edited this manuscript with great skill and kindness. Thank you for the insights that guided this book to a better conclusion.

Thank you to Charles and Maxine Hodges. My mother taught me to read and set the course for my whole education. My father taught me an appreciation for a good day's work. Carolyn Hardman was my favorite English teacher and taught me that there was great pleasure in reading and writing. I have always said that all anyone really needs is one good English teacher!

My brother and dear friend, Dr. Grant Hodges, patiently served as pastor of our church for thirty years, taught me to read Greek, and remains the one person on earth I would ask first about a question in the New Testament. Whenever I wanted to make sure that I was not straying off into the theological desert, he was the man I asked. Thank you is not enough.

Thank you to Robert Smith, M. D., who taught me the difference between victims and victors and who demanded that pathology be understood before we label people with disease. Thank you to Dr. Jay Adams who wrote *Competent to Counsel*, the first book I read in medical school that offered hope through biblical counseling to those who struggled emotionally.

I cannot remember who first told me that I should write a book about mood disorders, but Elyse and Phil Fitzpatrick have been consistent encouragers all along the way. Thank you for sticking with me!

Finally, as Paul wrote, "I am what I am by the grace of God." I thank God for giving me the privilege of writing a book.

Introduction:
Please Read Me!

When I set out to write *Good Mood, Bad Mood*, I intended to write about bipolar disorder to explain the explosive increase in the number of people who receive this diagnosis. But as I did the research, it became obvious that there is more to the issue than just explaining bipolar disorder. I found that the way we diagnose and treat depression is at the heart of the problem.

To understand bipolar disorder, we must understand the changes that have occurred in the diagnosis of depression. As a result, this book begins there and moves to the discussion of bipolar disorder in the following way:

Chapters 1–3 deal with the way our society views depression and examine the difficulties with the way the diagnosis is currently made. It seems as if everyone involved in the care of depression agrees about its cause and cure, but my research revealed much disagreement in the field. That important disagreement has been documented in the many footnotes that accompany the text. These notes are extensive but I hope they will serve as a valuable resource as you consider the role that depression has in our society.

Chapters 4–5 examine the way sadness has been confused with depression. This has resulted in "sadness over loss" being changed into the disease category of depression. This very significant change has been thoroughly documented as well. When sadness over losing things becomes a disease, it looks like an epidemic!

Chapters 6–13 examine the hope God gives us in his Word as we face struggles and sadness. Sorrow, anger, and worry are problems for which the Bible offers answers. We consider them in this part of the book primarily through a case study of one individual.

Finally, in chapters 14 and 15, we focus on bipolar disorder and the ways we can help those who have received this diagnosis. My hope is that this book will prove useful in clarifying the issues surrounding the diagnoses of depression and bipolar disorder and in presenting biblical ways to help those who suffer.

1

Making Choices, Looking for Hope

Most people do not enjoy being sick. I know there are a few who make a life's work out of their illnesses, but the rest of us could go a lifetime very happily without seeing a physician. I know this is true because I am a doctor. Most of my patients like me well enough, but they would rather run into me at church or the grocery store instead of my office. Some of them have medical problems that require them to come to my office several times a year and most of them do not look forward to it.

Usually, though, I can say that we help them. The medicine they take for their high blood pressure or diabetes makes a big difference in how long and how well they live. Unfortunately, it is not true for everyone. There are diseases we just don't have good answers for yet.

This has always been the case in medicine. Doctors are always looking for better cures. It was true when Jesus walked this earth. One case history illustrates the point. A woman had a problem that could not be cured with the technology and medication available at the time. Instead of having a simple monthly menstrual period, this woman had been hemorrhaging for twelve long years. Her story appears in three gospel accounts and Luke gives us the facts from a physician's viewpoint.

And a woman who had a hemorrhage for twelve years, and could not be healed by anyone, came up behind Him [Jesus] and touched the fringe of His cloak, and immediately her hemorrhage stopped.

—Luke 8:43–44

It had to be hard for a doctor to write that no one could help her. The woman had been cared for by many physicians, and not a one of them had an answer for her disease. It is tempting to say that Dr. Luke has been amazingly transparent here—until you read Mark's account of the same event.

Doctors typically avoid saying bad things about other doctors, but Mark was not a doctor. He described her as "a woman who had had a hemorrhage for twelve years, and had endured much at the hands of many physicians, and had spent all that she had and was not helped at all, but rather had grown worse" (Mark 5:25–26). Ouch! That was my thought as I read this as a physician.

This poor woman had not just been failed by the medical profession; she had "endured" much suffering. On top of that, she had gone broke paying medical bills and still was worse off than when she started! Admittedly, medicine was very primitive then. There were few medicines that worked and many of them, like mercury and arsenic, were poison. There were no x-rays, lab tests, or ultrasounds, but still, I wish my ancient colleagues could have helped her.

Instead, this woman found the help that only God could give her. She touched the hem of Jesus' robe and her bleeding stopped. The disease that had plagued, impoverished, and crippled her life for twelve long years was cured in an instant by the God who created her.

A Modern Parallel

Thankfully, medicine has made amazing advances since that woman was healed by Jesus. But we still face the same problem that doctors did in Luke's day. We encounter diseases that we struggle to accurately diagnose and effectively treat. And patients endure much. The purpose of this book is to look at another area of medicine in which patients face the kind of problems this woman faced. The diagnosis and treatment of the disease do not result in a rapid and complete cure. The cost of treatment and the lost wages are a significant burden to those affected. Yet in a significant number of cases, the real solution may be found in a meaningful encounter with the "Great Physician."

Mood disorders, including depression and bipolar disorder, have been at the center of health care in our country since the 1980s with the introduction of Prozac. We have spent billions of dollars to diagnose and cure depression, bipolar disorder, and related diseases. But the results are nearly as discouraging as they were with our first-century patient. The results for the diagnosis and treatment for mood disorders today are mixed.

Recent research would indicate that the current medical treatments do not seem to work well for many who are identified as depressed.[1] At the same time, there is concern that the way we make the diagnosis will apply the label of depressed to many who actually have emotional struggles but no disease.[2] There is also some indication that medicines may not be working as well as they did in the past.[3] Instead of finding a cause and cure for depression, we seem to be diagnosing more people with depression, but

[1] Jay Fournier, Robert DeRubeis, Steven Holton, Steven Hollon et al. "Antidepressant Drug Effects and Depression Severity," *Journal of the American Medical Association* 2010:303, (1):51. This study indicated that true drug effect was "nonexistent to negligible" for individuals with mild, moderate, and even severe depression. Only in "very severe depression" was true drug effect seen as compared to placebo.

[2] Alan Horwitz, "Creating an Age of Depression: The Social Construction and Consequences of the Major Depression Diagnosis," *Society and Mental Health*, 2011, 1(1) 41–54. Horwitz concludes on page 51 that the rapid increase in the rate of depression was better explained by changes in the criteria used to make the diagnosis rather than an increase in the prevalence of the disease.

[3] N. A. Khin, Y. F. Chen, Y. Yang et al. "Exploratory analysis of efficacy data from major depressive disorder trials submitted to the U. S. Food and Drug Administration in support of new drug applications," *Journal of Clinical Psychiatry*, 2011 Apr; 72 (4) accessed at *www.ncbi.nlm.nih.gov/pubmed/21527123* (accessed on 4/20/2012). This article indicated that the effect of placebos in drug trials had increased in the years 1983–2008 while "treatment effect clearly decreased."

with questionable benefit[4] and significant side effects.[5] One of my patients illustrates these problems.

Susan's Story

Susan[6] had begun to feel unwell nearly five years before she came to see me. She could not put her finger on what was bothering her at first, but she hurt in places she had never hurt before. She tried to ignore it but then worked her way through a succession of vitamins and glucosamine supplements. None of them seemed to help and, as a last resort, she decided to see her doctor.

Susan's family physician was a kind man with a good bedside manner. She did not run to the doctor for every ache and pain but, when she did go, Dr. Wilson always seemed to want to help. Usually a week's worth of some kind of medicine would have Susan back on track.

I wish I could say that Susan found the answer to her trouble during her first visit with Dr. Wilson. Instead she began a difficult search for relief from her pain. It began with blood tests, x-rays and ibuprofen that provided neither a diagnosis nor relief.

Dr. Wilson carefully worked through the likely causes of Susan's problems. After several visits Susan knew she did not have arthritis, lupus, ruptured spinal discs, hepatitis, chronic fatigue syndrome, or Lyme disease. The idea of fibromyalgia was entertained briefly, but she did not have enough of the specific tender points to meet the criteria. Like the man without a country, she moved from diagnosis to diagnosis for weeks.

After multiple visits, a pint or two worth of blood tests, and multiple MRIs, the defining moment of her life came in one of

[4]Alan Horwitz, "Creating an Age of Depression," 49. From 1987 to 1997 "the proportion of the U. S. population receiving outpatient therapy for conditions called depression increased 300 percent."

[5]P. Andrews, J. A. Thomson, A. Amstadter, M. Neale, *Primum non nocere*: an evolutionary analysis of whether antidepressants do more harm than good," *Frontiers in Psychology*, April 2012:3(117) 1–19. This is an excellent review of the current literature on depression. The authors state, "The weight of the current evidence suggests that antidepressants are neither safe nor effective." They do not say they should not be used but maintain that these medications should be used less.

[6]To avoid revealing any individual's medical history, Susan is a composite of several patients.

her many office visits with Dr. Wilson. I think I know how that doctor felt and what he must have been thinking. He had done every test he knew, considered every reasonable diagnosis, and tried multiple medications without much success. There were just two options left and Susan would have to make a choice.

After his diligent workup, Dr. Wilson believed that Susan was depressed and her pain was the result of a chemical imbalance in her brain. As sincerely and as kindly as he could, the doctor suggested that Susan either see a specialist for another opinion or take a new antidepressant as a trial to see if the diagnosis was correct.

The medicine would be free because Dr. Wilson had samples provided by the drug company. He hoped that in two weeks she would be better. What was there to lose? After hundreds of dollars in co-pays, Susan did not want to start over with another doctor and more tests. For a moment Susan hesitated, weighing the options.

As Susan did the calculations, she knew that Dr. Wilson cared and was well informed. He must certainly be telling her the truth. The medicine trial would be free since the manufacturer was providing samples. It gave her hope to think that after all the time and tests, she had something that could be treated.

So Susan chose to take the samples and begin treatment. Almost immediately she began to feel better. Dr. Wilson must be right! If all went well, in six weeks her pain would be a distant memory. Unfortunately, things did not work out that way. After six weeks, Susan believed she was somewhat better, but she now was contending with a new set of symptoms.

She found herself restless, with a feeling that she could not sit still. A new sense of anxiety gripped her. She now worried about things for no good reason. Instead of simply being concerned about her health, she worried about everything. Sleep began to elude her and her family and friends began to notice that she seemed on edge a lot of the time.

This prompted a return visit to Dr. Wilson with Susan's husband along. He was concerned about the changes he was seeing in Susan. He wanted to know more about what the doctor thought was wrong.

Dr. Wilson listened attentively to Susan and her husband and admitted that he was puzzled by the outcome of her treatment. She seemed to be doing so well at her follow-up visit, but he noted that sometimes some medicines don't agree with some patients. He offered to switch to a different drug from the same class and gave Susan samples. This seemed reasonable to Susan and her husband and they headed out the door with drug number two.

Sadly, Susan returned two weeks later because now she was struggling to sleep. Dr. Wilson noted that the medication could cause sleep disturbances. He offered to add a second drug at bedtime that would help. Now Susan was taking two antidepressants without feeling a great deal better than she did before the process started.

Six weeks later Susan returned, feeling much as she had on her previous visit. This time she came armed with information she had seen on television about a newer drug that could be added to the two she was already taking. She accepted the idea that she was depressed and it seemed reasonable that a newer, better medicine would help.

Dr. Wilson, however, was uncomfortable prescribing the new medicine. If Susan wanted to take the new drug, she would need to see a specialist. Again, Susan hesitated for just a moment. This was more than she had bargained for, but she feared quitting after investing so much time and money. She reluctantly agreed and Dr. Wilson referred her to a psychiatrist.

By this time, Susan was convinced that she had a disease that made her hurt, which was controlled by chemicals in her brain. She believed she could be cured if she just found the right medicine. And so she found herself in the office of Dr. Martha Smith, a psychiatrist and a genuinely nice person. Dr. Smith took a great deal of time examining Dr. Wilson's records and carefully discussed Susan's history and problems with her.

What came next caught Susan off guard. Instead of agreeing with her first diagnosis and writing the new prescription, Dr. Smith told Susan that she had a problem that seemed similar to depression but was really very different. Susan had a form of bipolar disorder (bipolar disorder II). This new diagnosis would account for her depression, irritability, restlessness, anxiety, and sleeplessness.

Dr. Smith told Susan that her parents most likely had passed this problem on to her. It was a lifelong problem that could never be cured, but could be treated with medication. Once she started the medication, she would need to take it indefinitely. If she followed the instructions, Susan could lead a relatively normal life. If she did not, she would continue to suffer.

Again, the hope of a new diagnosis and treatment was almost irresistible. It did seem a little strange to go from being a normal, healthy mother of three to being permanently sick with an inherited disease. But the doctor seemed to care a great deal about her and, as always, there were free samples to start the treatment. Once again, Susan chose to take the next step in the hope that this would be the answer.

Initially, Susan continued her original antidepressant and the new medication was added. Its potential side effects were considerable, including weight gain, diabetes, and involuntary jerking and tics. On top of that, Dr. Smith prescribed an anti-anxiety medicine to help with the side effects of the original drug. All of this should help her sleep, calm her down, and relieve her depression.

Susan was now six months into treatment, and she thought it was about time for things to get better. It would have been nice had it worked that way. Instead, Susan was back two months later to get started on a fourth drug. For the next four years, this process continued as new medicines and new combinations were tried. But life never did return to normal.

One day Susan realized that it had been five years since she began treatment and she was no better off than when she started. That day she made the most important decision of her life. Susan went back to her physician and asked her to arrange a vacation from her medicine. Susan wanted to know if the medicine actually made any difference. Her doctor reluctantly agreed and gradually weaned her off the medication.[7] (As a physician, I would add that

---

[7]No readers should consider stopping or changing their medication without first consulting their physician. Susan's story represents one person's experience and does not apply to all people and all medical problems.

Susan's decision to involve her doctor at this point was wise. No patient should stop taking his or her medicine or change the dose without first consulting the prescribing doctor.)

I met Susan a year later. At that time, she was continuing her vacation from medication and doing better. She still had some physical pain, but considered it less of a problem than the medicine she had been taking. She had recently moved to our area and was looking for a doctor in her neighborhood. She was emphatically not looking for new medication.

Susan's story is not uncommon. As a physician, I regularly see patients who could tell Susan's story because they are living it. They want to feel better and I want them to feel better too. They are diagnosed with bipolar disorder, depression, or anxiety. They take their medicine faithfully but continue to struggle. Their families struggle along with them as those who want to help. Everyone involved is looking for some hope that the pain and problems can be fixed.

Questions and Answers

Susan and patients like her resemble the sick woman who met Jesus. They are faced with pain that affects them physically and emotionally. In their search for a cure, they often see several physicians and have multiple tests done at considerable expense. They take multiple medications that may or may not help them. And, in the end, they may not be much better and may simply get worse.

The question I see in Susan's story is this: Could Jesus help her the way he helped the sick woman who touched his garment? Is it possible for the majority of people who struggle with mood disorders like depression and bipolar disorder to find help from God? Could that help be found in the Bible, where God speaks to us?

Another patient Jesus helped may point us to the answers to these questions. He was a crippled man who had waited to be healed or helped for thirty-eight years. The apostle John was the witness to this cure.

After these things there was a feast of the Jews, and Jesus went up to Jerusalem. Now there is in Jerusalem by the sheep gate a pool, which is called in Hebrew Bethesda, having five porticoes. In these lay a multitude of those who were sick, blind, lame, and withered, [waiting for the moving of the waters; for an angel of the Lord went down at certain seasons into the pool and stirred up the water; whoever then first, after the stirring up of the water, stepped in was made well from whatever disease with which he was afflicted.] And a certain man was there, who had been thirty-eight years in his sickness. When Jesus saw him lying there, and knew that he had already been a long time in that condition, He said to him, "Do you wish to get well?" The sick man answered Him, "Sir, I have no man to put me into the pool when the water is stirred up, but while I am coming, another steps down before me." Jesus said to him, "Arise, take up your pallet, and walk." And immediately the man became well, and took up his pallet and began to walk. Now it was the Sabbath on that day.

—John 5:1–9

There are no doctors involved here—just a sick man who had waited at the edge of pool, hoping that his superstition would make him well. The text inside the brackets is probably a late insertion, but it most likely represents what the man and most townspeople believed. Every once in a while an angel came and stirred the waters, but since the man was crippled, he couldn't get to the pool in time. Then one day Jesus walks by and asks if he would like to be healed. The man explains that he can't move fast enough to get there, but Jesus tells him to get up, take his bed and walk—and he did!

There are some interesting parallels to the problems we face with mood disorders today. Just like the man at the pool, we have a strong societal norm that says that if you are depressed or anxious, it is likely due to an abnormality in your brain chemicals, which can be cured by medication. Yet current research indicates that this theory may be no more certain than the hope of being cured by the troubled waters in the pool of Bethesda.[8]

---

[8]J. R. Lacasse, J. Leo (2005), "Serotonin and depression: A disconnect between the advertisements and the scientific literature," PLoS Medicine, 2(12):e392, www.plosmedicine.

Unexpected Hope

When Jesus told the crippled man to walk that command required him to give up on the idea of being cured by a treatment that had not worked. After thirty-eight years of disappointment, Jesus brought hope. The truth was that the man was never going to be healed by the conventional wisdom of his day. He was healed when he met Jesus who was and is the truth. Could the answer to mood disorders and anxiety be found in this same Jesus?

By some estimates, over 25 percent of the U. S. population will carry the label of depression, anxiety, or bipolar disorder at any given time.[9] Research indicates that less than a quarter of them will effectively gain a remission from depression as a result of the medication they take.[10] That leaves the rest, a significant majority, without a good answer for their problems and, most likely, without much hope.

That is what I have seen in the years I have practiced medicine. Some people who take the medication report that they feel better; others do not.[11] Questions and opportunities are raised by this. When many people do not improve, could there be a problem in the way they are being diagnosed and labeled? If that were so, it might explain why many people do not seem to benefit from the

org (4/29/12). 1212–1213. The authors state that "contemporary neuroscience research has failed to confirm any serotonergic lesion in any mental disorder and has in fact provided significant counterevidence to the explanation of simple neurotransmitter deficiency. . . . To our knowledge, there is not a single peer-reviewed article that can be accurately cited to directly support claims of serotonin deficiency in any mental disorder." PLoS Medicine is the online medical journal of the Public Library of Science.

[9]NIMH: Statistics for anxiety disorders and all mood disorders. Accessed electronically at www.nimh.nih.gov/statistics . The annual prevalence of anxiety disorders is estimated by the National Institute of Mental Health to be 18.1%. The lifetime prevalence is 28.8%. Annual prevalence for depression is 9.5% and lifetime is 20.8%. (4/29/2012)

[10]J. Blumenthal, M. Babyak, M. Doraiswamy et al. "Exercise and Pharmacotherapy in the Treatment of Major Depressive Disorder," *Psychosomatic Medicine,* 2007; 69 (7):587–596. This study showed that those treated with sertraline, exercise, or placebo responded to treatment with remission in 47% of the patients in the sertraline group, 41% of the exercise group, and 31% of the placebo group. In this study, when the placebo effect is subtracted from the medication group, the real effect is 17%.

[11]The presence of a response to a medicine does not always mean that there is disease present, nor does it mean that the medicine caused the cure. Viral colds and penicillin are a good example. A lack of a response to a medicine also does not mean that there is no disease present. Things related in time are not always related by cause.

medication. What percent of those who struggle with sorrow and a depressed mood have a medical problem? The most important question has to be: Is there anything more we can offer people to give them hope? To answer these questions and take advantage of the opportunities, three areas need to be explored.

Defining the terms. The first step to finding hope for people identified with bipolar disorder, depression, or anxiety is to have a clear understanding of what those terms mean. There is often a big difference between the way a patient understands bipolar disorder and the way it is described by physicians and psychologists. The same can be said for depression and anxiety. As we look for hope, we will examine the history of these diagnostic labels and what they mean today.

Understanding the diagnostic process. The second step will be to examine how a diagnosis of depression or bipolar disorder is made and the label assigned. Many things influence this process. It is important to understand how a physician or psychologist decides that someone has this (or any) disease.

The biblical alternative. Over the last twenty years, there has been a major effort to educate people about depression. The main tenet of that education is that depression and mood disorders are medical problems that require medical treatment. When most people feel depressed today, they go to the doctor in search of a medical answer. Today very few would go to their pastor first and few caregivers would view the Bible as relevant to the problem.

In the third step, we will look at the ways the Scriptures offer help and hope to people who carry these labels. They have most likely already been to the doctor and gotten the same result Susan did. I believe there is comfort and direction available for anyone who has been labeled bipolar, depressed, or anxious like Susan. This applies to those who take medication and those who do not.

One of our current societal norms for mood disorders and depression is to either relate it or equate it to pain. As a current television advertisement for a popular antidepressant says, "Depression hurts."[12] The commercial makes a strong visual argument that when we hurt physically and there is no clear cause, it may be depression.

Ed Welch reflects the idea that depression hurts in his book, *Depression: A Stubborn Darkness*, when he says, "Depression is painful."[13] That is how we see depression inside and outside the church. When people struggle with a depressed mood, they do hurt emotionally, and the pain they feel spreads to every corner of their lives, touching all who know and love them. Things today are much the same as when Jesus was touched by the suffering woman and when he told the crippled man to walk. Then and today, the pain and suffering are real and people want help.

While almost no one I know makes it his goal in life to be depressed, bipolar, or anxious, thousands of people carry those labels with them every day. They struggle with the burden of the label and the pain of their problems. This book aims to help them find the kind of help that Jesus wants to give to those who see him as their last and only hope.

---

[12]Eli Lilly television advertisement for Cymbalta. This advertisement can be seen on youtube at http://www.youtube.com/watch?v=OTZvnAF7UsA. It was copyrighted 7/02/2009. (5/03/2012) The theme of the advertisement is that depression hurts and that the hurt is depressed mood, lack of energy, lack of interest, anxiety and other symptoms common to depression.
[13]Edward T. Welch, *Depression: A Stubborn Darkness* (Winston-Salem, N.C.: Punch Press, 2004), 37.

2

Where Did Susan's Diagnosis Come From?

When I think about Susan and her experience with the health care system, one thing that sticks in my mind is the confusion about what disease she had. There was Susan, struggling to feel better and to know what her problem really was, and the best my profession could do left her confused and suffering. How could there be so much confusion and difference of opinion about the diagnosis of a disease?

It's easy to understand why physicians failed to make a good diagnosis for the suffering woman Luke described. Physicians of that day had little or no understanding of human anatomy. The role of bacterial infection in disease was not understood. The importance and purpose of blood was unknown. In our day MRIs, CT scans and ultrasounds give us pictures we could only imagine thirty years ago and none of it existed in the first century. The woman Luke described—and those who tried to help her—were hindered by a lack of objective scientific information to make a diagnosis and provide treatment.

It is hard to believe that the same thing could be true today for people diagnosed with depression, bipolar disorder, or anxiety. But, in light of Susan's long, unsuccessful quest for medical help, isn't it possible that doctors and patients, like Susan, lack the kind of information about pain, worry, and depressed moods that is needed to help them? Unfortunately, people who suffer with depression, wild mood swings, and worry *do* face the same problem. The diagnosis of these emotional disorders is much more difficult and far less certain than something like diabetes or a strep throat.

When a patient comes to my office complaining of a sore throat, fever, and a headache, the odds are that my nurse will have made the diagnosis before I enter the exam room. She will do a rapid strep screen from a swab of the throat. A positive test means that the patient will be taking penicillin for about ten days. A negative test means that the patient probably has a virus and does not need an antibiotic. All of that can be determined with one test in about eight minutes.

Even more complicated medical problems can be diagnosed in a matter of hours instead of days. A patient who presents with a headache and new visual changes may have a migraine headache. He could also have a brain tumor. Today, in a couple of hours, I can have the patient in a CT-scanner to determine with absolute certainty whether he has a tumor or not.

Diagnosing Depression

I wish I could say that medicine can make a diagnosis that easily for people suffering emotional distress. It would be so helpful to be able to do a test that would help us relieve their burdens. But the test does not exist. In fact, there are no laboratory tests or x-rays that can make the diagnosis of depression.[1]

---

[1] *Diagnostic and Statistical Manual of Mental Disorders, Fourth Edition, Text Revision* (Arlington, Va: American Psychiatric Publishing, 2000), 352. This manual is currently being revised a fifth time. "No laboratory findings that are diagnostic of a Major Depressive Episode have been identified." The key to the quote is the word "diagnostic." There are

What we do have are criteria that must be met—a list of symptoms that must be present—in order to make a diagnosis of depression. Those criteria are found in the *Diagnostic and Statistical Manual of Mental Disorders*. For someone to be given the diagnosis of depression, five or more of the criteria must be present for two weeks and must represent a difference in the person's behavior.[2]

From the list of nine criteria, either a depressed mood or a loss of interest in pleasurable pursuits must be present. The symptoms cannot include any that are caused by a medical condition, delusions or hallucinations.

The list includes:

1. A depressed mood daily for most of the day, nearly every day, as indicated by subjective report or the observation of others.

2. A loss of interest or pleasure in all activities for most of the day, nearly every day.

3. Weight loss or gain of more than 5 percent of body weight due to an increase or decrease in appetite.

4. Inability to sleep normally or excessive time spent sleeping daily.

5. Visible restlessness and agitation or sluggishness and slowing down as seen by others.

6. Fatigue or loss of energy daily.

7. Feelings of worthlessness or guilt without a reason.

8. Decreased ability to think, concentrate, and make decisions.

9. Recurring thoughts of death, or suicide without a plan. Suicide attempts or plans for suicide.

---

tests that could be said to be suggestive but to this day there are none that have been validated as diagnostic.

[2] *Diagnostic and Statistical Manual of Mental Disorders*, 356.

DSM IV
Major Depressive Episode

A. Five (or more) of the following symptoms have been present during the same 2-week period and represent a change from previous functioning; at least one of the symptoms is either (1) depressed mood or (2) loss of interest or pleasure.

Note: Do not include symptoms that are clearly due to a general medical condition, or mood-incongruent delusions[1] or hallucinations.

(1) depressed mood most of the day, nearly every day, as indicated by either subjective report (e.g., feels sad or empty) or observation made by others (e.g., appears tearful). Note: In children and adolescents, can be irritable mood.

(2) markedly diminished interest or pleasure in all, or almost all, activities most of the day, nearly every day (as indicated by either subjective account or observation made by others)

(3) significant weight loss when not dieting or weight gain (e.g., a change of more than 5% of body weight in a month), or decrease or increase in appetite nearly every day. Note: In children, consider failure to make expected weight gains.

(4) insomnia or hypersomnia nearly every day

(5) psychomotor agitation or retardation nearly every day (observable by others, not merely subjective feelings of restlessness or being slowed down)

(6) fatigue or loss of energy nearly every day

(7) feelings of worthlessness or excessive or inappropriate guilt (which may be delusional) nearly every day (not merely self-reproach or guilt about being sick)

(8) diminished ability to think or concentrate, or indecisiveness, nearly every day (either by subjective account or as observed by others)

(9) recurrent thoughts of death (not just fear of dying), recurrent suicidal ideation without a specific plan, or a suicide attempt or a specific plan for committing suicide

B. The symptoms do not meet criteria for a Mixed Episode.

C. The symptoms cause clinically significant distress or impairment in social, occupational, or other important areas of functioning.

D. The symptoms are not due to the direct physiological effects of a substance (e.g., a drug of abuse, a medication) or a general medical condition (e.g., hypothyroidism).

E. The symptoms are not better accounted for by Bereavement, i.e., after the loss of a loved one, the symptoms persist for longer than 2 months or are characterized by marked functional impairment, morbid preoccupation with worthlessness, suicidal ideation, psychotic symptoms, or psychomotor retardation.

---

[1]A mood congruent delusion exists when a depressed person believes a false idea that fits with his mood. He is depressed and he believes the world is ending. A mood incongruent delusion is seen when a depressed person believes a false idea that does not fit his mood.

For someone to be diagnosed with depression, these symptoms must cause real distress, problems with family and friends, and trouble at work. The symptoms cannot be the result of substance abuse or any medical condition. They should not be the result of grieving over the loss of a loved one. If they are, the problems must last longer than two months.

The Problem of Over-Diagnosis

Most people would agree that people who report the symptoms listed certainly sound like they have a depressed mood. It seems straightforward enough in theory. The physician, mental health professional, or counselor asks the patient if she has these problems and to what degree. The problem is that, in practice, this diagnostic approach is not nearly as accurate as a blood glucose test or a rapid strep screen. There are subjective assessments being made by both the patient and the health care provider.

In fact, the current method of diagnosing people with depression is known to label more people with major depressive disorder than actually have it. In the words of Gordon Parker in the *British Medical Journal*, "Reasons for the over-diagnosis of depression include lack of a reliable and valid diagnostic model. . . ." Simply put, the criteria we use simply do not work well.[3] The problem is that "DSM-III's operational criteria were set at the lowest order of inference." This means that the bar to justify a diagnosis of depression was set so low that almost anyone could meet it at some time in life.

In order to qualify, you only have to report that for two weeks you have been sad, blue, or down in the dumps. You would also need to have a change in appetite, sleep disturbance, fatigue and a drop in libido.[4] In a study conducted by Parker starting in 1978 with 242 teachers, 95 percent reported emotions consistent with a depressed mood around six times a year. When the same group was revisited in 1993, 79 percent of the group had "met the criteria for major, minor, or subsyndromal depression" as defined in the

---

[3]Gordon Parker, "Is Depression Over-Diagnosed? Yes," *British Medical Journal*, 335 (August 18, 2007) 328.
[4]Ibid., 328.

DSM. This is a very high percentage of people to qualify for the diagnosis of depression.

The problem with these criteria as a diagnostic tool is that they include feelings and experiences that almost everyone has in the course of normal life. Far too many normal things are said to be indicators of a disease according to these criteria. The National Institute of Mental Health currently estimates that during our lifetimes 20.8 percent of us will be labeled as depressed.[5] But as we saw above, the Parker study group, using the DSM criteria to diagnose depression, reported a figure of nearly 80 percent. What would happen if the diagnostic standard for pneumonia included everyone who coughs? You would have a lot more people diagnosed with pneumonia—wrongly. If you lower the standard for diagnosis, you increase the number of people who qualify for it. The suggestion that the criteria used for depression might be inflating the numbers of people diagnosed is not new. Parker is not alone in his criticism.

Jerome Wakefield concluded in a March 2010 article in the *American Journal of Psychiatry* that a criterion added to reduce the number of false positive diagnoses did not help at all. Wakefield said that a normal person faced with serious loss may develop a depressed mood that could last longer than two weeks *without* having a disease that required treatment.[6] He believed that some other alteration of the criteria was needed in order to reduce "false positive diagnoses" in depression. The real problem seems to be that the "test" most commonly used to diagnose people with depression is flawed. It cannot distinguish between grief that lasts more than

---

[5]NIMH Statistics: Any Mood Disorder, *National Institute of Mental Health, www.nimh.nih. gov/statistics* (4/29/2012).

[6]Jerome Wakefield, "Does the DSM-IV Clinical Significance Criterion for Major Depression Reduce False Positives? Evidence from the National Co-morbidity Survey Replication," *American Journal of Psychiatry* (2010) 167:298–304. www.ajp.psychiatryonline.org (5/9/2012). The problem was that ". . . diagnosis and the need for treatment are not the same. Intense normal reactions to loss and stress can include distress [and] role impairment . . . that can transiently resemble disorder." The criterion was the requirement that symptoms cause significant distress and impairment. A second qualifier exists for bereavement, which extends the period that a person can be emotionally distressed after the loss of a loved one from two weeks to two months.

two weeks and a real disease because it lacks a means to validate or confirm the results.[7]

As a physician, I wish I could say that the problem is only with the test. The truth is, not only are the criteria flawed but most of the time physicians simply don't use them when they diagnose depression. This is the psychiatric equivalent of omitting the rapid strep screen on a sore throat. A full quarter of psychiatrists admit that, more than half the time, they do not use the DSM-IV criteria when they make a diagnosis of depression.[8]

It is even worse among primary care physicians, my part of the profession. Among primary care doctors, two-thirds admit that they don't use the criteria half the time.[9] To complicate matters further, primary care physicians think they are better at diagnosing depression than they really are. One study asked physicians how they rated their ability to gauge the severity of a patient's depression. This is very important, since the severity often dictates the treatment. In the study, 55 percent of the physicians thought they were good at rating the severity of depression. In reality they were right around 60 percent of the time, which made them only slightly better than a coin flip.[10]

So when it comes to depression, the queen of mood disorders, confusion reigns. The medical profession may have good intentions, but when Susan and many like her go looking for relief, they are in much the same fix as the woman in the Gospels. Without a way to make a reliable diagnosis, physicians do not know exactly what they are treating.

---

[7]T. Richard Manne, "Too Many People Misdiagnosed with Depression: Blame the Criteria or the Doctors?" *Science 2.0* (March 10, 2010) *www.science20.com* (5/9/2012). We will deal with the issue of validity in chapter 5.

[8]Mark Zimmerman, "Psychiatrists' and Non-psychiatrist Physicians' Reported Use of the DSM-IV Criteria for Major Depressive Disorder," *Journal of Clinical Psychiatry* 2010; 71(3):235–238.

[9]Ibid., 235.

[10]Ingrid Olsson, Arnstein Mykletun, Alv A. Dahl, "General practitioners' self-perceived ability to recognize severity of common mental disorders: An underestimated factor in case identification?" *Clinical Practice & Epidemiology in Mental Health.* 2:21 (2006) *PubMed Central, http://www.ncbi.nlm.nih.gov/pmc/articles/PMC1560123/* (5/10/2012).

That leads to the experience Susan had. When her originally diagnosed mood disorder did not respond to the care she was given, Susan was diagnosed with another mood disorder, using another set of criteria. Unfortunately for her and her physicians, there was and is no objective test that can make a diagnosis of bipolar disorder II easy or certain. Again Susan found herself answering a list of questions about her behavior.

Elusive Criteria

The criteria for the kind of bipolar disorder Susan was supposed to have are as follows:[11]

1. One major depressive episode is required.

2. One period of hypomania is required. This is defined as an elevated mood in which she had more energy, was disorganized, had racing thoughts, irritability, anxiety, insomnia, and agitation. To make things even more uncertain, the mood could be negative *or* positive. During hypomanic episodes, patients may complete more work than usual. Hypomania should not be confused with euthymia, a short period when the depression lifts and the individual feels emotionally normal.

3. The individual has never had mania or been diagnosed with bipolar disorder I.

4. The episodes cannot be better explained by a general medical illness, adverse reaction to medicine, substance abuse or another psychiatric disorder such as schizophrenia.

One would hope that the diagnosis of BPD could be made more easily and accurately than that of depression, but that is not the case. There are two reasons for this that are similar to the problems involved in diagnosing depression. First, in order to receive a diagnosis of bipolar disorder, an individual must have an episode of

---

[11] *Diagnostic and Statistical Manual of Mental Disorders*, 392.

major depression, and we have seen how that diagnostic process is fundamentally flawed. Then, the same subjective approach is used to diagnose the required episode of hypomania.

As with depression, there are no laboratory, x-ray or physical findings that help physicians to make this diagnosis. We simply have a list of behaviors that are supposed to be observed. We ask patients about these behaviors using a questionnaire or by taking their medical history. As Susan found out, the likelihood that a patient will be given a label that does not help him is great. Physicians who really want to help lack an accurate and reliable tool to use. Patients risk receiving a diagnosis that may be inaccurate, leading to treatment that does not help.

There can be no doubt that most physicians enter medicine because they want to help people. None of us like to read about patients who have the wrong knee replaced or who suffer ill effects because the wrong medicine is given. I frequently remind my students that doctors do not get up in the morning thinking of ways to hurt people! No, they dedicate a significant portion of their lives to study, hard work, and sleepless nights to learn a profession that allows them to help.

That being so, why does it seem that we are trapped with a diagnostic process that labels so many without helping them? Physicians seem to be hampered by the way they decide if someone is depressed or has bipolar disorder. How did we get into this fix? Understanding how we got here is the first step for getting out of the label trap.

I have practiced medicine for thirty-seven years. I am old enough to say with conviction that we have not always diagnosed most diseases the way we do today. In most cases this represents progress, in that tests are quicker and more accurate now. The way we diagnose mood disorders has also changed, but it remains a difficult thing. A short look at the history of how we make that diagnosis might help us understand the problems we face today.

The Changing Description of Mood Disorders

The history of depression and bipolar disorder is a complicated one because for the last 200 years, the diagnosis of mental disorders has largely been a matter of "expert" opinion. And there were lots of opinions that gave us labels like circular insanity, cycloid psychosis, and folie circulaire.[12] Without objective evidence such as laboratory, x-ray, or even physical exam findings, the diagnosis of mood disorders was made using a history of the patient's behavior and his family history. This is still true for most mental disorders, except for those connected to medical diseases that can be detected through objective tests, such as hyperthyroidism and Cushing's disease.[13]

After 1900, the "art and science" of medicine took a hard turn towards science. Discoveries in scientific areas such as chemistry were finding their way into the practice of medicine. As a result, the medical profession became more objective. With William Perkin's discovery of dyes that could stain cells and Paul Ehrlich's use of those dyes, medicine was on its way to becoming a profession based on facts.[14]

Ehrlich gave medicine and psychiatry an amazing gift when he took the purple dye Perkin developed and used it to stain tissue samples from patients with various kinds of diseases. His colleagues did the same in the Charite mental hospital in Berlin. Ehrlich and his colleagues examined the stained tissue under the microscope. They discovered that half the residents who had been judged as "simply" insane actually were suffering from infectious diseases that had damaged the brain.[15] One simple, objective test provided a factual result that changed the course of medical history. Medicine was beginning the march toward verifiable, repeatable, factual evidence as the basis for the diagnosis and treatment of disease.

[12]For a very good history of the diagnosis of mania, see *Mania: A Short History of Bipolar Disorder* by David Healy (Baltimore: Johns Hopkins Press, 2008).
[13]Appendix B discusses medical diseases that affect mood and behavior.
[14]Gary Greenberg, *Manufacturing Depression* (New York: Simon and Schuster, 2010), 44–49. This is an excellent history of the birth of modern medicine.
[15]Greenburg, *Manufacturing Depression*, 48–58.

While medicine in general was busy defining disease in as factual a way as possible, psychiatry at the time had only the personal observations of practitioners and the theories that grew from their observations. By 1950, psychiatry was seeking a vocabulary that would enable it to be more scientific as well. The new terminology first appeared in a classification of disease written by Emil Kraepelin in 1893.[16] This book suggested no treatments because Kraepelin did not believe that the diseases he described could be treated. But Kraepelin's book gave physicians caring for mental patients a common language to use in identifying the behavior they were seeing.

In 1952, the psychiatric world witnessed the publication of the first Diagnostic and Statistical Manual of Mental Disorders. This reference work was not intended to be a re-creation of the Kraepelin text, but in some ways it was just that. The DSM did not dictate the best way to treat or even diagnose all the disorders listed in its pages. However, it did offer an agreed-upon description of each "disease" and the criteria that had to be met for someone to qualify for the diagnosis. (It also provided a code that was required for the psychiatrist or other provider to bill for services.)

In 1980, the term bipolar disorder appeared in the DSM 3rd revision in place of manic depression.[17] The purpose was to clarify the difference between manic depression and schizophrenia. But there was more to it than that. At the same time, the committee added the categories of bipolar disorder II, cyclothymia, and bipolar disorder NOS (not otherwise specified). The NOS category allowed psychiatrists some "wiggle room" to diagnose patients with bipolar disorder who might not meet the whole standard. This made it easier to label a patient as bipolar.

Before this change was made, a patient had to be hospitalized with a life-disrupting episode of mania to be given a diagnosis of manic depression or bipolar disorder I. This made the diagnosis of manic depression much simpler—and much less frequent. But

---

[16]Greenburg, 71–74.
[17]David Healy, "The Latest Mania: Selling Bipolar Disorder." *PLoSMedicine* 3:4 (2006) 3 www.plosmedicine.org (3/28/2012).

now physicians and psychologists were given less specific criteria and several more options to consider in making the diagnosis.

The end result is that people with very dissimilar problems wind up with the same labels: depression and bipolar disorder. And a lot more people are assigned those labels. Susan was one of millions in our country to be diagnosed with depression or bipolar disorder and then treated medically.

Many of these individuals have one more thing in common with Susan: they receive little benefit from their diagnosis or their treatment. In the January 2010 issue of the *Journal of the American Medical Association*, a large study found that in patients with mild, moderate, and even severe depression, a placebo had the same therapeutic benefit as an active antidepressant medication.[18] Depending on the study, patients in these three categories make up 70 percent to 87 percent of all patients who present with depression.[19][20] The study concluded that unless a person had very severe depression, a placebo pill was as effective as antidepressant medication.[21] Even when treating very severe depression, the placebo effect could account for up to 80 percent of the effect of the antidepressant medication.[22]

There are many ways to interpret this information. Perhaps the first point is that this does not mean that no one is helped by the medicine available to treat depression today. Even if less than 10 percent of those who take the medicine are helped, we should be

[18]Jay Fournier, Robert DeRubeis, Steven Hollon et al. "Antidepressant Drug Effects and Depression Severity: A Patient-Level Meta-Analysis," *Journal of the American Medical Association*, 303:1 (January 6, 2010) 51. "True drug effects (an advantage of antidepressant medication over placebo) were non-existent to negligible among depressed patients with mild, moderate, and even severe baseline symptoms. . . ."

[19]Mark Zimmerman, Michael Posternak, Iwona Chelminski, "Symptom Severity and Exclusion from Antidepressant Efficacy Trials," *Journal of Clinical Psychopharmacology*, 22:6 (December 2002) 610–614. In this study 70 percent of those presenting with depression were considered mild, moderate, or severely depressed.

[20]Sharon Begley, "Anti-Depressants Don't Work, Do Work: The Debate Over the Nation's Most Popular Pills," *Newsweek* (February 8, 2010) 39.

[21]Fournier, "Antidepressant Drug Effects," 51.

[22]Irving Kirsch, Brett Deacon, Tania Huedo-Medina et al. "Initial Severity and Antidepressant Benefits: A Meta-Analysis of Data Submitted to the Food and Drug Administration," *PLoS Medicine*, 5:2 (February 2008) 266. www.plosmedicine.org (5/13/2012).

glad for them. The second point would be that no one should stop taking or adjust their medication without first consulting their physician. But the third and (I would argue) most significant point is that the current approach to the diagnosis and treatment of depression fails to help a large portion of those who need it.

Medical researchers continue to look for a way to identify a physiological cause for depression and we should be glad they are. When Paul Ehrlich and his colleagues were busy staining cells, the result was that the number of people diagnosed with insanity dropped by half.[23] Truth is never an enemy in the pursuit of understanding and curing disease. A real understanding of the cause of depression, at the cell level, would allow an accurate, repeatable test. It would greatly reduce inaccurate over-diagnosis.

Ehrlich put it best when he said, "It should be possible to find artificial substances which are really and specifically curative for certain diseases, not merely palliatives acting favorably on one or another symptom. . . ."[24] As things stand today, we have not reached that goal for the diagnosis and treatment of depression. We certainly lack the tests, and the medicines are far less effective than had been hoped.

For Susan and those like her within the 87 percent who do not seem to benefit much from current treatment, it means that they may still suffer the same fate as the woman with the hemorrhage in Jesus' day. The labels they receive and the prescriptions they are given might only result in more labels and prescriptions without a cure and at some expense. This opens a door of opportunity for us to look at depression from a different angle.

Even in a nation with the best health care on earth and the best doctors in history, the labels may be wrong and the treatments may not work well. It has been that way for as long as physicians have

---

[23]Greenberg, *Manufacturing Depression*, 57. "By one count, nearly half of the patients in Europe's mental hospitals were suffering from tertiary syphilis." The symptoms of untreated late syphilis were interpreted as insanity at the time.

[24]Ibid., 53. After identifying spirochetes as the cause of syphilis, Ehrlich set out to find a chemical compound to kill them and cure patients of syphilis. On his 606th attempt, salvarsan, an arsenic compound, was found to kill the organisms and cure the disease, and the course of medicine changed forever.

tried to diagnose and treat disease. At times we are wrong, and changing those wrong ideas has proved to be hard. But it is time for us to do just that. We can assume that a small portion of those who fit the current criteria may have a medical disease whose cause is yet to be discovered. But while we wait for that discovery and better treatment, we could be doing something for the 87 percent who don't seem to benefit from current diagnosis and treatment.

Instead of assuming that everyone with a depressed mood has a disease that requires medical treatment, it could be that we are looking at people who are simply sad for a variety of identifiable reasons. If we are going to help those who struggle with mood disorders, we need to have a better understanding of what is or is not a disease. In the next chapter, we will examine a few ideas that should help us distinguish sadness from disease.

3

Disease or Not?

So far we have seen that the problems Susan faced were intensified by a system that failed to understand her trouble. The diagnostic tools were just not up to the job. While Susan struggled with her pain, her doctors wrestled with tools that were not always reliable. The lack of a clear diagnosis put them all in a no-win situation. What they needed was factual information that would result in a diagnosis that could be understood and treated.

There are a number of very real and serious diseases that come with a disturbed mood.[1] They include things like hypothyroidism, hyperthyroidism, Cushing's disease, Huntington's disease, and pancreatic cancer. It is very important that those ills be identified and properly treated. At the same time, there are also serious problems in life that affect our moods but have nothing to do with medicine or disease. Distinguishing between the medical and non-medical causes of our bad moods can save lives in either case.

When we decide that our ache, pain, sad mood, or worry is caused by a medical malfunction, our options are limited to medi-

---

[1] Appendix B deals with physical illnesses that change both emotion and behavior.

cine. If we choose not to make that assumption, we can look for other explanations of our troubles.

Disease or Not?

Part of the answer to Susan's problem may be found in the way doctors usually make a medical diagnosis. While I was in medical school, I saw an example of the way this can go wrong. I met a physician who was nationally known for his description of a syndrome. He had spent his whole life treating myasthenia gravis, a neurological disease with a definite pathology and treatment. He was a good physician and well respected for his work, but his undoing would be pathology.

Pathology is defined as the study of the essential nature of diseases, especially the structural and functional changes they produce in the body.[2] No disease exists in the human body without some kind of change at the cell level, which results in an abnormal function. We may know exactly what the pathology is, as we do in diabetes. We may not know exactly what it is, as in migraine headaches. But in both cases pathology exists. Physicians and medicine do their best work when we know the pathology. But we sometimes get lost without it.

Over time, the physician whose specialty was myasthenia gravis became convinced that he could help another group of patients who had similar symptoms but did not meet the pathology criteria for the disease. That is, tests did not reveal the changes in tissues and organs that are seen in myasthenia gravis (with the resulting changes in bodily function). For these patients, the doctor invented the term myesthenoid syndrome. Eventually, he stayed very busy treating this group of people using expensive medications normally used to treat myasthenia gravis.

He became so busy, in fact, that it was said that if you put a black mark on a map for every patient diagnosed with myesthenoid syndrome, Indiana (where this doctor practiced) would look like a

---

[2]Merriam-Webster's online dictionary, http://www.merriam-webster.com/medical/pathology (5/14/1012).

black island in the middle of a sea of nothingness. In other words, no one diagnosed this disease but him! The doctor was convinced about his diagnosis and his patients were too, but his syndrome had no objective scientific evidence to support its existence. There simply were no changes in organs or tissues to confirm his diagnosis. Recently, I did a web search for myesthenoid syndrome and found nothing. The disease has disappeared along with the doctor who diagnosed it because it was not a real disease.

This doctor took a disease he was familiar with, which could be diagnosed using laboratory tests, and morphed it into something else. He was convinced he was right because his patients seemed to get better when they took medicine. The same reasoning convinced the patients. They took the pill, they felt better, and therefore they believed they had a disease.

Pathology Is the Gold Standard for Disease

The problem with myesthenoid syndrome is the same problem the doctors faced in trying to help Susan. She had been given diagnostic labels that included anxiety, depression, and bipolar disorder II, but none of these have symptoms that can be consistently measured objectively by physical findings, x-ray imaging, or laboratory testing. This makes the diagnosis a matter of opinion.

Now, opinion is part of medicine and it can be a valuable element in diagnosis. When we don't like the first opinion we get, we often will seek a second. But those opinions must be based on fact if they are going to help us. When physicians give opinions based only on their perceptions (based on personal experience and not reproducible fact), we end up with a diagnosis like myesthenoid syndrome. The only way to avoid this kind of confusion is to look for pathology—that is, for specific, negative changes in organs, tissues or systems.

The dictionary definition of disease is "a pathological condition of a part, organ, or system of an organism resulting from various causes, such as infection, genetic defect, or environmental stress, and characterized by an identifiable group of signs or symptoms."[3] Pathological here means that when that portion of the body is examined by some objective means, you can see a change in the tissue.

Disease is best defined by objective means. A headache could indicate a brain tumor and a CT scan will show it. A patient with a headache and a normal scan does not have a brain tumor. If his blood pressure is high at 220/120, then the blood pressure is the cause. The scan and the blood pressure provide the doctor with objective findings. Susan's problems had none of the features that would meet the standard definition of disease,[4] and we would not expect her to have any. In the words of the DSM, "No laboratory findings that are diagnostic of a Major Depressive Episode have been identified."[5] In other words, no physical findings are specific to or diagnostic of depression.

Not all disease can be defined by pathology, but most of it can be. For some diseases, the source of the problem may be hidden in the brain, as in the case of migraine headaches. Right now, our tests are not sophisticated enough to pinpoint their cause. The pathology exists but we cannot identify it. We often use the terms "syndrome" or "disorder" when we are dealing with a physical problem but cannot identify the malfunctioning cells causing the problem. We had no broken or malfunctioning cells to point to as the cause of Susan's problem. I believe that gives us the freedom and even the obligation to look at her symptoms differently.

Truth Sets People Free

In medicine, the presence or absence of pathology—negative changes in a tissue, organ, or system—is very much like the presence or absence of truth. Patients with normal blood glucoses do not have diabetes. When your tissue biopsy returns normal, you do not have cancer. The importance of "pathological" truth came into clear focus in 1983 when a physician and a pathologist from Australia rocked the medical world by declaring that peptic ulcer

[3]American Heritage Dictionary, retrieved from www.answers.com on 2/3/2007.
[4]*Diagnostic and Statistical Manual of Mental Disorders*, 349–351.
[5]Ibid.

disease was not caused by emotional stress or by excess acid produced by nervous stomachs.

For fifty years, two generations of physicians were taught that the pain and burning of peptic ulcers were the result of the patient's inability to deal with the struggles of life. In medical school we learned the catchy dictum, "It's not what you are eating, it's what's eating you!" Armed with bottles of Maalox, antispasmodics, and Valium, we did our best to help those with ulcers. Unfortunately, it was hard to say whether anyone taking two tablespoons of Maalox every two hours was better off than someone who just suffered with the disease.

All of this treatment depended on a fifty-year-old study done by Hans Selye.[6] He demonstrated that if you subject rats to anything that causes great pain, they develop stress ulcers in their stomachs. His conclusion was that this was also the cause of stress ulcers in people, which required a considerable leap of faith since no such study could be done with humans. But despite the lack of human studies to demonstrate the pathological connection, modern medicine made that leap.

Most of the patients we cared for with peptic ulcer disease seemed to be "stressed." And some of them seemed to improve when we dealt with their stress and reduced their stomach acid. The problem with that line of reasoning lay in the fact that people who live with constant stomach pain had a good reason to be nervous; their stomachs hurt and the treatment was not very comforting. It did not necessarily mean that stress was the original cause.

Those who did not improve or who developed bleeding ulcers faced surgery that was not very helpful either. Then came Tagamet. This drug offered hope of treatment but no cure.

But then in the fall of 1983 at a conference in Belgium, Drs. Barry Marshall and Robin Warren presented a paper that would change all of this. They had discovered a pathological explanation

[6]Hans Selye, "GAS Spells Stress," *Brain Connection,* http://brainconnection.positscience.com/topics/?main=fa/selye (5/15/2012). Hans Selye was a noted endocrinologist who initially believed that stress or strain could lead to physical problems such as peptic ulcer disease. I was taught his viewpoint in medical school in the 1970s.

for peptic ulcer disease—and neither stress nor stomach acid had anything to do with it!

The doctors found the bacteria *helicobacter* growing in the biopsy specimens taken from the stomachs of peptic ulcer disease patients during stomach endoscopies.[7] Marshall told the conference that the cause of peptic ulcers was infectious disease, not stress or gastric acid. It could be cured by eight dollars worth of amoxicillin and a bottle of Pepto-Bismol taken for two weeks. Considering how bad the treatment of ulcers had been to that time, he should have received a standing ovation.

Instead, the young doctor was met with skepticism. He was described as a crazy guy saying crazy things. Underneath all the criticism was the spectacular amount of money being spent in research by companies dedicated to the proposition that gastric acid caused peptic ulcers. But Marshall was saying that getting rid of gastric acid would control but not cure peptic ulcers.

For several years Marshall struggled to prove his findings because he could not experiment on humans. Finally, in 1985 he resorted to the time-honored practice of experimenting on himself. Like Robert Louis Stevenson's Dr. Jekyll, Marshall took a flask of liquid that was growing the bacteria *helicobacter* and drank it. In a week he developed an inflammation of his stomach called gastritis. He took the ridiculously inexpensive antibiotic for two weeks and was cured. He had provided the objective, reproducible scientific data to support his claim.

Organized medicine was still unconvinced, but doctors in the U. S. read about Marshall and began to treat patients with amoxicillin and Pepto-Bismol. After all, what could two weeks' worth of penicillin and Pepto hurt? The outcome shook the foundation of medicine right down to its gastrointestinal assumptions. Patients who had suffered for decades were cured in two weeks.

By 1994, Marshall's "theory" that *helicobacter* was the infectious cause of peptic ulcers became the accepted truth. It became accepted

---

[7]A procedure in which a physician introduces a hose-like instrument into the stomach to look at the stomach lining. This allows the physician to make a diagnosis and take samples for pathologic examination.

truth because Marshall and Warren had the pathology findings to prove it. In 2005, Marshall and Warren received the Nobel Prize in medicine for their work. Of the whole experience Marshall said, "Everyone was against me, but I knew I was right."[8] Marshall reminds us that truth sets people free. For Susan, the truth was that there was no evidence of pathologic change in her body that could explain her pain or any of the problems that followed. The explanation that her pain was due to depression (and eventually bipolar disorder) was developed from a theory, not objective facts acquired with scientific testing. Everyone along the way meant well, but the outcome was still very much like Hans Selye and peptic ulcer disease.

Looking for the truth by relying on objective physical data will do one of two things. (1) It can point us to the correct medical diagnosis and eventually a treatment that cures or comforts. (2) It can also tell us that since there is no scientific evidence of a physical problem, there is no current medical explanation for the patient's symptoms and we should look elsewhere.

There was also another factor that affected Susan's situation. The theory upon which her diagnosis and treatment were based had research evidence problems very much like Hans Selye's rodent experiments.

Chemical Imbalances and Real Pathology

Most of the treatment Susan received was guided by the chemical imbalance theory, which has been widely used to explain the physical origin of mood disorders such as depression and anxiety since the early 1980s. The concept is simple. In 1965, Joseph Schildkraut proposed that depression was caused by a deficit of norepinephrine in the brain. Others proposed that a deficit of serotonin was the cause.

---

[8]Academy of Achievement Interview with Dr. Barry Marshall. The quote is found on page 8 of the interview. Last revised on September 23, 2010. http://www.achievement.org/autodoc/ printmember/mar1int-1 (5/14/2012). It is an amazing story of perseverance in the face of great academic opposition, well worth the reading. He knew he was right because he had the pathology.

It was believed that the behavior and emotions of depression were caused by an imbalance between certain chemicals in the brain, including norepinephrine, dopamine, and serotonin.[9] The theory became the centerpiece of a decade-long educational program promoted by the manufacturers of selective serotonin reuptake inhibitors (SSRIs) such as Prozac and Zoloft.

Definitions from the Pharmacy

Serotonin, norepinephrine, and dopamine are chemicals that are involved in the normal function of the brain. In theory, a lack or excess of these chemicals is supposed to be the cause of emotional disorders like depression.

SSRI stands for *selective serotonin reuptake inhibitors*. These are a class of medicines that are supposed to increase the level of serotonin in the brain in order to treat depression and other emotional disorders.

A *placebo* is a pill or treatment that appears to be real though it has no real drug in it. It is used in research to determine if an actual dose of medicine helps a disease or if the patient's improvement is due to his belief that the medicine will help.

Pfizer, Inc. ran ads that were famous for making the chemical imbalance theory simple. Those who were depressed did not have enough of the little "balloons" containing serotonin in their brains. Zoloft was said to increase the level of serotonin by increasing the number of balloons. The ad concluded by saying that "Zoloft works to correct this imbalance."[10]

The average viewer or reader would conclude that depression is a disease caused by a chemical imbalance in the brain and medicine could correct the problem. That, however, was not entirely true.

Realizing the Chemical Imbalance Theory Is Unproven

There are many significant problems with the chemical imbalance theory, and they are key to understanding the way diagnoses of

---

[9]Jeffrey Lacasse, Jonathan Leo, "Serotonin and Depression: A Disconnect between the Advertisements and the Scientific Literature," *PLoS Medicine*, 2:12 (December, 2005) 2, www.plos. org. (3/4/2006).
[10]J. Lacasse, 2.

mood disorders have increased and evolved in recent years. The first problem is that the chemical imbalance theory of depression is just that—a theory. While the lay literature and the public statements of drug manufacturers seem to indicate that this theory is scientific fact, there has never been a peer-reviewed, published journal article that proves that a serotonin deficiency is the cause of any mental disorder. Further, even today we do not know what the correct balance of serotonin, dopamine, or norepinephrine should be in the human brain.[11]

On the contrary, research has shown that depression could not be consistently induced by reducing serotonin levels or relieved by large increases in serotonin. Instead of correcting an imbalance (as Pfizer ads asserted), SSRI medicines may create an abnormal state in the brain that patients prefer to the symptoms of depression.[12]

Newer medications also are casting doubt on the chemical imbalance theory of depression. Currently in France, a medication is being used to treat depression that is supposed to lower the level of serotonin. Tianeptine is a selective serotonin reuptake enhancer that has the same ability to reduce the symptoms of depression that the SSRI Prozac-type antidepressants are supposed to have.

This drug has the exact opposite action of the reuptake inhibitors by increasing the reuptake of serotonin into the nervous system cells. Yet it still reduces the symptoms of depression to about the same degree.[13] Since the chemical imbalance theory was based on the idea that serotonin was too low, it is nearly impossible to construct an explanation for the theory when a medication that lowers serotonin helps depression.

The popular life of the chemical imbalance theory has been about fifty years—somewhere near the length of time that Hans Selye's ideas about stress and peptic ulcers persisted. And, towards the end, it wasn't Selye who was promoting it. Long after Selye ceased to think that there was a circulating hormone secreted under stress

[11]J. Lacasse, 4.
[12]J. Moncrieff, D. Cohen, "Do Antidepressants Cure or Create Abnormal Brain States?" *PLoS Medicine* 3:7, July 2006, 961. May be found at www.plosmedicine.org .
[13]Irving Kirsch, *The Emperor's New Drugs* (New York: Basic Books, 2010), 97.

that caused ulcers, there were people like me in medical schools being taught some of the tenets of his theory.

The chemical imbalance theory is suffering the same fate. While it was not a particularly bad idea, it simply lacked any scientific evidence to prove it existed. And today researchers are abandoning it as quietly as we quit prescribing Maalox when a better diagnosis and cure was discovered. A number of researchers have spoken to this issue. "Although previously the monoamine systems were considered to be responsible for the development of major depressive disorder (MDD), the available evidence to date does not support a direct causal relationship to MDD. There is no simple direct correlation of serotonin or norepinephrine levels in the brain and mood."[14]

That sounds a lot like a scientific obituary and that author is not alone. Another researcher of note is Thomas Insel, a psychiatrist who directs the National Institute of Mental Health. Of the chemical imbalance theory Insel said, "There is no biochemical imbalance that we have ever been able to demonstrate."[15] In fifty years of trying, we still do not have one well-documented study that gives us the smoking gun for the chemical imbalance theory.

And science is moving on. Insel also said, "What we think about are changes in circuitry and how the brain processes information," and his agency is funding research in cognitive therapy.[16] It is as if we are watching the chemical imbalance theory get smaller in the rearview mirror while science drives away.

Irving Kirsch, the associate director of the Placebo Studies group at Harvard Medical School, has this to say about the chemical imbalance theory. "The biochemical theory of depression is in a state of crisis. The data just do not fit the theory."[17] The validity of the theory is important to anyone who either gives or receives care

---

[14]H. Ruhe, N. Mason, A. Schene, "Mood Is Indirectly Related to Serotonin, Norepinephrine and Dopamine Levels in Humans: A Meta-Analysis of Monoamine Depletion Studies," *Molecular Psychiatry* 12 (2007): 331–359.

[15]Stacey Burling. "How do controversial changes in psychiatry's guidebook make you feel?" *Philadelphia Inquirer* (May 5, 2012) 3. http://articles.philly.com (5/6/2012).

[16]Ibid, 3.

[17]Irving Kirsch, *The Emperor's New Drugs*, 98.

for depression. A faulty theory will lead to faulty treatment. But, even more important, when a theory is held to be true, it shapes our thinking about how to respond to the problem. Knowing that the chemical imbalance theory is not fact drives us to look elsewhere for better answers as physicians and counselors.

However, there is one argument left in support of the theory. It is strongly defended and the hardest to refute. People who take antidepressants get better! When patients are presented with statistical evidence that indicates that the medicine might be less than effective, their response is their own story: "I felt terrible. I took the medicine. It made me feel better. I must have a disease and the medicine works." The argument boils down to something like this: If I have a disease, take medicine, and recover, it proves two things. (1) I have a disease and (2) the medicine works.

Medicine usually rejects this kind of reasoning to support a diagnosis or treatment. It is called ex juvantibus or "reasoning 'backwards' to make assumptions about disease causation based on the response of the disease to a treatment."[18] I recently read an editorial written by a psychiatrist who was responding to questions about the effectiveness of antidepressants. His response was his own heartrending story. His sister died at the World Trade Center on 9/11 and two weeks later he said, "My body gave out."[19] He told how he tried most everything to help his depression and then took an antidepressant and recovered. His conclusion was that "antidepressants have been shown to work. . . ."[20]

It is difficult to argue against a story like that and, frankly, who would want to do so? But, in truth, it is anecdotal—one man's story—and in medical science we avoid making conclusions based on one man's story. We avoid it because it leads us to treat viral sore throats with penicillin because the patient felt better, or to treat warts with duct tape because they went away. In both cases, had

[18]J. Lacasse, "Serotonin and Depression," 3.
[19]Sharon Begley, "Anti-Depressants Don't Work, Do Work: The Debate Over the Nation's Most Popular Pills," *Newsweek* (February 8, 2010), 42.
[20]Ibid.

we done nothing or had we done something different, the problem still would have gone away.

The latest developments in the study of depression indicate something entirely different from the psychiatrist's assertion. The real issue is not whether or not antidepressants are effective and therefore prove that depression is a disease. Instead, it is why the medication works at all. Surprisingly, this really is not a new question.

For at least ten years, there has been a growing awareness that the antidepressants we have, including the newer SSRI Zoloft/Prozac types, have not worked as well as hoped. In an article published in the *Journal of the American Medical Association* in 2002, researchers compared St. John's Wort, Sertraline (Zoloft), and a placebo look-alike pill.

They found that the antidepressants gained a full remission of depression in 25 percent of patients, while St. John's Wort (an herbal remedy) did so in 24 percent of patients. The findings were stunning since they indicated that an inexpensive over-the-counter herbal remedy worked as well as an expensive medication. But the most interesting part of the study was that the placebo worked better than both, with nearly 32 percent of the patients getting over their depression.[21] More research reported in 2002 not only confirmed these findings but raised more questions about the effectiveness of antidepressants.[22]

In research that examined forty-seven studies of antidepressants conducted or sponsored by the makers of the medicines, Irving Kirsch found that 82 percent of the benefit of taking them came from placebo effect. In over half the studies, published and unpublished, the antidepressants worked no better to relieve depression than the placebo did[23] and in 87 percent of patients with depression, the difference between the active drug and placebo was "nonexistent."[24] What does this mean? Again, a placebo is a time-honored

---

[21]Hypericum Depression Trial Study Group, "Effect of Hypericum Perforatum (St. John's Wort) in major depressive disorder: A randomized controlled trial," *Journal of the American Medical Association* 287, no. 14 (April 10, 2002) 1807–1814.

[22]Sharon Begley, "Antidepressants Don't Work . . . ," 36.

[23]Begley, 36.

[24]Begley, 39.

method of determining whether or not a treatment actually does anything for a patient who uses it. In such studies, patients are divided into two groups, with one group receiving the active drug being studied. The second group receives a pill that looks like the first but contains no medicine.

The simple message from these studies was that in 82 to 87 percent of those treated, the drugs themselves were not the source of the benefit. The greatest benefit came to those who believed in the drug and gained hope from that belief. This presents an enormous challenge to the argument that depression is a disease because the "medicine made me feel better." If a sugar pill can "cure" the disease as well as the real drug 82 percent of the time, then we cannot be certain of the benefit of the "real" pill, and we cannot use the "cure" as an argument to prove the chemical imbalance theory.

There are many ways to interpret this information. One conclusion you can safely draw is that when you take medicine and get better, it does not necessarily mean that you have a disease. Medicine has always been plagued by the reality that things that happen at the same time are not always related by cause. As we just noted, warts and viral sore throats are two examples of this problem. When placebos perform as well as they do, antidepressants can't claim that their effectiveness proves that depression is a disease.

We are also under no obligation to believe that mood disorders are caused by a chemical imbalance or that currently available medication can affect that balance. The scientific evidence is not there to prove either statement. It may be true that these medicines work for the very seriously depressed (13 percent of all those affected),[25] but even that is not entirely certain. What does appear likely is that for nearly 90 percent of the 30 million people diagnosed (or 27 million) there is no true chemical benefit.[26] That would mean that eight billion of the nine billion dollars spent last year on these medicines may have been spent in vain.

---

[25]Begley, 39.
[26]Hypericum Depression Trial Study Group, "Effect of Hypericum Perforatum (St. John's Wort) in major depressive disorder: A randomized controlled trial,"1807.

This leaves us with no solid scientific data to identify the causes of mood disorders or to prescribe appropriate care. People who have made this argument have been met with the same kind of skepticism and criticism that Barry Marshall suffered. But, just like Marshall, we are free to look for a better answer.

There are many places to look. Given the fact that nine billion dollars are spent every year on antidepressants, it is certain that research will continue to try to identify the cause and cure of mood disorders. But if there are 27 million Americans who are helped just as much by their hope for relief, maybe it would be good idea to look at the role hope plays in medicine for just a moment.

Hope as an Active Ingredient in Medicine

In July 2002, a study was published in the *New England Journal of Medicine* that dealt with the fascinating relationship between doctors and hope in medicine. At the time, 650,000 knee surgeries were being done for arthritis of the knee and the question was whether or not the 3.5 billion dollars it cost was actually helping patients.[27] What the study found was that the surgery made no difference or significant improvement in how the knees functioned. But there was something in the study that was far more interesting.

The surgeon was a brave soul and he decided that there would be three groups in the study. One group would have the standard, extensive surgery done, while a second would have a less aggressive procedure. A third group would have nothing done to the knee. The patients in the third group would be put to sleep and superficial incisions made to resemble those made in the real surgery, and then sewn up. This created the placebo group.

The results were startling. When patients were questioned about pain relief, there were significant differences in the outcomes among the three groups. Those who had the most extensive surgery saw a reduction in the pain scale at two weeks of around 8 percent; at two years it was about the same. Those who had the minimal procedure

---

[27]Bruce Moseley, Kimberly O'Malley, Nancy Petersen, "A Controlled Trial of Arthroscopic Surgery for Osteoarthritis of the Knee," *New England Journal of Medicine*, 347:2 (July 11, 2002) 81–88.

had pain relief of 12 percent at two weeks and 3 percent at two years. The patients who had the placebo procedure (no real surgery at all) had a 19 percent reduction in the pain scale at two weeks and at two years still had an 11 percent reduction over baseline.[28]

The fact that the placebo group had better pain relief than the surgical groups is tied to two things. First, they had no surgery to cause pain and second, they had great confidence in the care of the surgeon. They had hope. There is a similarity between this and the St. John's Wort study. In both studies the placebo group did best probably because in both cases there were no side effects from the medicine or the surgery.

Hoping in Something Besides Medicine

The question that comes to my mind is: Is there any place besides medicine where we can look for hope for those with mood disorders? It turns out that there is a lot of hope to be had. In recently reported research, believing in God appears to be a great way to reduce stress and anxiety. Even better, believing in a God who cares about you makes medical treatment 75 percent more likely to work among the clinically depressed. The researcher said "that it was specifically tied to the belief that a Supreme Being cared."[29] If antidepressants work no better than a placebo, and a belief in a loving, caring God makes the treatment work better, it could be that the real help is not going to be found in medicine.

Two thousand years ago, the caring, concerned Son of God, Jesus Christ, announced the solution to our mood struggles. It was revolutionary. It did not involve medicine and, considering the primitive state of the healing arts at the time, that was a very good thing. It was completely non-commercial. No one would profit from any cure, and no one would have a conflict of interest. It simply required the struggler to look at trouble in a different light.

To the anxious, Jesus said,

---

[28]Bruce Moseley, "A Controlled Trial of Arthroscopic Surgery for Osteoarthritis of the Knee," 85.
[29]Jennifer Harper, "Studies: Belief in God Relieves Depression," *Washington Times*, Feb. 25, 2010. Retrieved electronically at www.washingtontimes.com.

"And who of you by being worried can add a single hour to his life? And why are you worried about clothing? Observe how the lilies of the field grow; they do not toil nor do they spin, yet I say to you that not even Solomon in all his glory clothed himself like one of these. But if God so clothes the grass of the field, which is alive today and tomorrow is thrown into the furnace, will He not much more clothe you? You of little faith!

"Do not worry then, saying, 'What will we eat?' or 'What will we drink?' or 'What will we wear for clothing?' . . . For your heavenly Father knows that you need all these things. But seek first His kingdom and His righteousness, and all these things will be added to you."

—Matthew 6:27–33

To those with illness and pain, Jesus said, "For whoever wishes to save his life will lose it; but whoever loses his life for My sake will find it. For what will it profit a man if he gains the whole world and forfeits his soul? Or what will a man give in exchange for his soul?" (Matt. 16:25–26).

To those who struggle daily with the darkest moods, Jesus said, "Blessed are those who mourn, for they shall be comforted"(Matt. 5:4). To gain comfort, human beings would have to look at the problems of life differently and to respond to them the way Jesus did. Jesus said to His disciples, "If anyone wishes to come after Me, he must deny himself, and take up his cross and follow Me" (Matt. 16:24).

And if people choose to think and act in a radically different way as they face the struggles of life, Jesus offers something that most of us are looking for and cannot find. "Come to Me, all who are weary and heavy-laden, and I will give you rest. Take My yoke upon you and learn from Me, for I am gentle and humble in heart, and you will find rest for your souls. For My yoke is easy and My burden is light." (Matt. 11:28–30).

The initial path Susan followed did not give her rest, nor was it easy. It consumed five painful years of her life. The choices offered to those with mood disorders by modern medicine should not prevent Susan and those like her from looking elsewhere—especially when the opportunity to look at our troubles differently is real and the burden of looking is light. We have nothing to lose but our heavy burdens.

The rest of this book will look at the path the Bible presents to deal with the struggles often at the heart of mood disorders. We will examine how the Great Physician's prescription can help.

4

Jesus, Suffering, Sadness, and Hope

When Susan first visited her doctor, she went seeking an explanation for her pain. She certainly did not consider herself depressed. What drove the process through doctors, diagnostic labels, and medications was her discontent over not feeling good. Susan wanted to feel good and that required a diagnosis. When none could be found, it affected her mood. As Susan struggled with the idea that she might never feel normal again, she developed a sad sense of hopelessness.

Susan was like many people I meet who must deal with depression and the diagnoses that follow when medical care does not relieve their distress. They lack hope. Christians who suffer in the dark mood of depression are often doubly troubled. They have their sad mood and their doubts. Why do they have to suffer? Where is God in all of this? Why do they have to deal with this hopeless darkness?

I can think of no better place to find the answer to such suffering and sorrow than the account of the illness of Lazarus in the gospel of John. It is a familiar story because of the ending.

Now a certain man was sick, Lazarus of Bethany, the village of Mary and her sister Martha. It was the Mary who anointed the Lord with ointment, and wiped His feet with her hair, whose brother Lazarus was sick. So the sisters sent word to Him, saying, "Lord, behold, he whom You love is sick."

—John 11:1–3

Lazarus was not just any man. He was the "certain man" because Lazarus, Martha, and Mary were dear friends of Jesus, who stayed in their home when he was in Bethany. You and I might have expected Jesus to jump and run when he heard that message. But instead, really strange things happen. First, Jesus does not run to his friend's aid. His first response is to say that "this sickness is not to end in death, but for the glory of God so that the Son of God may be glorified by it" (11:4).

That was really well worded. If you know the end of the story, you know that Lazarus is dying. The disciples will miss the point, as do most of us. As Lazarus is dying, Jesus stays where he is for two more days. Then he announces that it is time to go and wake Lazarus from sleep. His disciples are not keen to make the trip because the Jews want to kill Jesus—and them. They thought the sleep would do Lazarus good.

Then Jesus makes the most remarkable statement on human illness and suffering in Scripture: "Lazarus is dead! And I am glad!" (11:14–15). Try preaching that at a funeral, as you look down at the departed and the grieving family. "Fred is dead and I am glad!" You'd be lucky to escape from the church or funeral home unscathed. But there is an end to Jesus' sentence. "I am glad for your sakes . . . so that you might believe" (11:15). Jesus is saying, "My friend is dead, his sisters suffer, but you and a bunch of other people are going to believe!"

In that moment the curtain is drawn back and we get to see why other believers have suffered. Jesus knew all about Lazarus and that he had died. Jesus Christ, the Son of God, had a plan that, in the long run, was going to be better than the one that Martha, Mary, or Lazarus had. But then there was one more question: Did Jesus, the friend of Martha, Mary, and Lazarus, care? Or were they just expendable pawns? That question is important to us, because we ask it in the middle of our suffering. Does he care?

Does Jesus Care?

So off Jesus goes, but he takes his time. When Jesus finally arrives, Lazarus had been in the grave four days. Consider that and enter into the suffering of Lazarus and his sisters. I suspect that the messenger was paid to run to Jesus and it did not take two days to reach him. The message was urgent. Every day, Jesus' three friends waited for him to come over the hill. Then it was just Martha and Mary. You can feel the hope leak out of their lives with each passing second. Then Lazarus dies and hope is nearly as dead as he is.

Then word comes to Martha that Jesus is here. She always was the practical one and she runs with a mission. "Lord, if you had been here my brother would not have died" (11:21). Those are hard words to say and hard words to hear. "Lord, where were you when we needed you?"

But Martha was still on a mission. She really did not need to know why; she just wanted to know if Jesus would help.

Martha keeps right on talking. Even now, as dead as Lazarus is, "I know that whatever You ask of God, God will give You." Jesus answers, "Your brother will rise again!" Martha misses it. "I know that he will rise again in the resurrection on the last day" (11:22–24).

Then Jesus says, "I am the resurrection and the life; he who believes in Me will live even if he dies, and everyone who lives and believes in Me will never die." Then Jesus asks Martha the question on which everything in life hangs. "Do you believe this?" (11:25–27). I wonder how long the question hung in the air.

Jesus has told her that he has a plan for Lazarus, one that is better than the one she had when she sent the messenger: "Please, come quickly, Jesus, and heal my brother while he is alive!" That was her plan and Jesus did not fulfill it. Now, four days later, Jesus wants to know, "Do you believe this?" Martha responds, "Yes, Lord" (11:27).

Martha goes in to tell Mary that her Lord is here. Mary runs out and says the same sentence: "Lord, if you had been here my brother would not have died." She falls at his feet weeping.

Then we see the answer to the question: Does God care? Did Jesus care? If he cared, why did he let this good man die? Jesus looks at

Mary and the family and he weeps. As the hymn affirms, "Oh yes, he cares, I know he cares, his heart is touched with [their] grief."[1]

So Jesus knew, Jesus had a plan, and it would be a better plan than Martha's. It would result in people believing and God being glorified. Jesus cared deeply about the loss that Martha, Mary, and Lazarus suffered. But it did not stop there. It did not stop with Jesus knowing or Jesus caring.

When the Weeping Is Over: Hope!

After Jesus had wept, he instructed the people, "Remove the stone." Martha objects because it had been four days. Martha had given up. She had submitted her will to what she thought Jesus' plan was—to leave Lazarus in the tomb until the second coming. But that is not the plan. Jesus says, "Did I not say to you that if you believe, you will see the glory of God?" (11:40). Jesus is telling her, I have a better plan!

> So they removed the stone. Then Jesus raised His eyes, and said, "Father, I thank You that You have heard Me. I knew that You always hear Me; but because of the people standing around I said it, so that they may believe that You sent Me." When He had said these things, He cried out with a loud voice, "Lazarus, come forth."
> —John 11:41–43

Lazarus did just what Jesus ordered and it changed everything.

There are people who will read this whose problems are just as desperate as this. The burden they must carry has crushed hope out of their lives. They have pursued relief from their emotional and physical problems with physicians who want to help them as much as they want to be helped. Yet they still struggle in the darkness of a depressed mood without hope.

There is hope for those who have not found help even though they have looked for it diligently. In the same way that Jesus cared for a poor woman with an untreatable medical problem, Jesus

---

[1] Frank Graeff, J. Lincoln Hall, "Does Jesus Care?" *Worship and Service Hymnal* (Carol Stream, Ill.: Hope Publishing, 1985), 377.

cares about us when we suffer. In the same way that Jesus cared for Lazarus and his sisters, he cares for us.

As we face trouble ourselves or try to help others, we can have hope because we know a few things for certain:

First, we know that Jesus knows about our problems in the same way he knew about Lazarus. Nothing can happen to us that escapes his attention. "For the LORD knows the way of the righteous, but the way of the wicked will perish" (Ps. 1:6).[2]

Second, we can have hope because we know that Jesus has a plan for our problems just as he had a plan for Lazarus. Though the plan was not obvious to the disciples or his friends, Jesus had one. Just as God had a plan for Israel as they suffered exile in Babylon, Jesus had a plan for Lazarus that was for his "welfare and not for calamity, to give you a future and a hope" (Jer. 29:11). We know that the plan Jesus has for our trial is better than any plan we can design.

Third, we can have hope because we know that Jesus cares about our problems. Since Jesus wept for his friends, we know he can "sympathize with our weaknesses." As we suffer we know that he has suffered and was "tempted in all things as we are, yet without sin." We can have hope because we can ask Jesus, who knows our problems, for help. We can come "with confidence to the throne of grace, so that we may receive mercy and find grace to help in time of need" (Heb. 4:14–16). We can come just like Martha and expect mercy and grace!

Fourth, when Martha and Mary both ask Jesus, "Where were you when we needed you?" Jesus does not answer them with a rebuke. In the middle of our own struggles, I somehow think God expects us to wonder why we have them. Jesus did not say to Martha, "How dare you question me?" Instead, he told her that he was going to raise Lazarus from the dead and she would see his glory. When Mary said the same thing, Jesus wept. We can have hope in the middle of depression because we know we have a God

---

[2] Psalm 1:6. The writer contrasts the believer and the unbeliever. Christians can depend on God knowing their troubles. Non-Christians do not have that benefit. Appendix A explains how to become a Christian and how to have the assurance that God knows and cares about our problems.

...ten to our cries with a sympathetic ear, just as he did
...and Mary.

...d Purpose in Sadness

...t comfort for the sad, struggling Christian in the way
... Martha, Mary, and Lazarus. The story raises a greater
...for us. What is the purpose or value of sadness?
...live in a nation dedicated to the idea that no one should
...needlessly sad or depressed for any prolonged period of time.
Our government has spent millions of dollars to tell us this and
to identify people who meet the criteria of depression. Additional
millions are spent each year on television commercials by phar-
maceutical companies, aimed at convincing us that this pain and
sadness can and should be fixed.

Billions have been spent on medication to rescue those who
suffer this sadness from a miserable existence. In an educational,
economic, and public policy sense, it seems that we have voted
with our dollars to end sadness that lasts more than two weeks. As
we seek to avoid the pain depression brings, a question comes to
mind. If Jesus was willing to let his friends suffer as they did, why
don't we see suffering as valuable?

I don't think we are medically capable of banishing sadness and
depression from our lives, but if we were, should we want to do
it? Is there anything to lose by doing so? Would we be giving up a
part of our humanity, intended by God to be used the same way it
was for Martha, Mary, and Lazarus? Could it be that never being
sad would leave us spiritually impoverished?

The Bible has much to say about sadness, sorrow, and suffering.
The characters in its pages were well acquainted with the experience. Today, even outside the circles in which the Bible is faithfully
consulted, there are people who deal with depression who are asking
the same questions. They, too, wonder if much depression is not just
normal sadness or grieving. They also think we may need it. In the
next chapter we will see sadness and depression from their viewpoint.

5

Depression or Sadness:
Two Ways to Consider the Diagnosis

Most everyone involved in trying to help depressed people would say that Susan fit the criteria in the DSM-IV. They would also have agreed with the treatment she received. They probably would have been disappointed, but not shocked, that she did not benefit much from her medication. They would view Susan's problems as unfortunate and they would continue looking for the right combination of medicine to dispel her depression.

They would tell Susan that some people respond to one kind of medication better than others. The important thing for Susan would be to stick with the process until the right doses of the right medicines could be found. If she were patient while her doctors made those adjustments, eventually she would feel better.

Unless the diagnosis was wrong.

In their book, *The Loss of Sadness: How Psychiatry Transformed Normal Sorrow into Depressive Disorder*, Alan Horwitz and Jerome

Wakefield offer a reasonable explanation for Susan's experience.[1] The reason nothing seemed to help Susan very much in those five years was simple. She was not depressed.

This is not to say that she was not sick. It certainly does not mean that she did not have real physical pain or that she was not suffering. Like the woman with the hemorrhage, Susan suffered much. She had a sad mood and looked at life in a miserable way. But she was not depressed. Susan was, as Horwitz would say, "normally sad."[2]

"Normal Sadness" versus Depression

"Normal sadness" is something that happens to most of us when we lose something very important to us. In other words, the sadness fits the situation. The onset and duration are connected to the problem the individual must face. Susan's illness would qualify. A physical ailment that just won't get better is a good enough reason to be sad. The loss of a loved one, a job, a prized possession, a pet, or the failure of a marriage or important friendship all fit the mold. Anything we lose that we value highly can be the source of normal sadness.[3]

A second feature of normal sadness is that the intensity and duration of our sadness corresponds to the size and duration of the loss.[4] The loss of a new baby to disease or accident can bring enormous grief that can last a lifetime. The loss is huge and it is, in relationship to this life, permanent. Getting a traffic ticket might make some cry, but generally the sadness is short. It is not a great loss and it passes quickly. For the sadness to be normal, the loss must be real and not a delusion or hallucination. Susan's physical pain was real and significant. It stayed with her long after she abandoned the idea of being depressed.

A third aspect of normal sadness is that it goes away when the problem goes away. It also ends when the individual "adapts" to

---

[1] Alan Horwitz, Jerome Wakefield, *The Loss of Sadness: How Psychiatry Transformed Normal Sorrow into Depressive Disorder* (New York: Oxford University Press, 2007).
[2] Ibid., 19.
[3] Horwitz, *The Loss of Sadness,* 43.
[4] Ibid., 43.

the problem.[5] The man who is sad because he lost a job recovers quickly when he finds work. The man or woman devastated by the end of a romance may struggle, but a new relationship generally lifts the sadness. The family that loses a teenaged son to a car wreck can find some measure of solace knowing that his heart saved the life of someone else's child. Susan eventually decided to respond differently to her pain and found relief from her sad mood. In these cases, either the problem was resolved or the individual was able to adapt to it.

Disordered Sadness

If Susan was really normally sad, then we have to ask: What exactly is depression? This has never been an easy question. Prior to 1980, it meant different things to different people. The confusion was great enough that the diagnosis a patient received depended on the physician he or she chose to consult.[6] There was a lot of subjectivity involved. However, most people agreed that there was an important difference between sadness that came with adversity and sadness that appeared without any cause.

The latter came to be known as disordered sadness and is mentioned by Hippocrates, the father of medicine, and by Aristotle.[7] Both indicated that disordered sadness or melancholia (as they would name depression) came without a reasonable cause and stayed far too long. This view of depressive, melancholic sadness would be affirmed by many.

Cotton Mather wrote, "These Melancholicks do sufficiently afflict themselves . . . they make themselves as Miserable, as they could be from the most real miseries."[8] Benjamin Rush, a signer of the Declaration of Independence and considered the father of

---

[5]Ibid., 43.

[6]D. L. Rosenhan, "Being Sane in Insane Places," *Science,* Vol. 179 (January 1973) 250–258. This is interesting research in which normal individuals went to mental hospitals to play the part of an "insane" patient and were diagnosed with mental disorders.

[7]Horwitz, 76.

[8]Cotton Mather, "How to help Melancholicks." In J. Radden, *The Nature of Melancholy: From Aristotle to Kristeva* (New York: Oxford University Press, 2000) 161–165. Mather's original work was published in 1724.

American psychiatry, also spoke of melancholia. He noted that melancholics struggled with emotion that was "disproportioned in its effects, or its expected consequences, to the causes which induce them."[9]

In the twentieth century, it would be hard to find anyone more important than Sigmund Freud[10] and Adolph Meyer[11] in psychiatry. Both affirmed the importance of context in the diagnosis of depression, as did most everyone in the field until 1980. In that year, a momentous change occurred that completely altered the way depression is diagnosed.

The DSM's Inadequate Criteria

This event set in motion one of the most significant changes in health care in my lifetime and it would be at the center of Susan's difficulty. At the heart of the change and the controversy are the criteria used to diagnose Susan's depression. The problem is that the tools given to us by the creators of the DSM—the nine criteria discussed in chapter 2—are unable to distinguish between normal and disordered sadness.

Instead, after the symptoms of depression (including sadness) have been present for two weeks, the DSM criteria identify the problem as depression. No consideration is given as to whether the symptoms are caused by an identifiable problem. The only exception is bereavement and even that is only supposed to last for two months. This aspect of the criteria was included with good intentions.[12]

The DSM's goal was to establish a set of symptoms that everyone would agree fit the diagnosis of depression, no matter what theory of depression they embraced. The purpose was to insure that when one psychiatrist labeled a patient with depression, the next psychologist or social worker would agree. The 1980 DSM criteria

---

[9]Benjamin Rush, "Hypochondriasis or Tristimania," In J. Radden, *The Nature of Melancholy*, 211–217. Rush's original work was published in 1812.
[10]Horwitz, *The Loss of Sadness*, 94.
[11]Ibid., 104.
[12]Ibid., 71.

came into existence under the guidance of Robert Spitzer. They were written so that it made no difference how you thought people became depressed as long as they met the criteria.[13]

Reliability, Specificity, Sensitivity, Validity

This approach enabled those who used the criteria to achieve statistical reliability. That is, the questions they asked (based on the DSM criteria) would "reliably" elicit the same answers from those who were depressed. Patients who exhibited symptoms of depression would all be asked the same questions. Those who answered them in ways that matched the criteria would be diagnosed with depression; those whose answers did not meet the criteria would not be. The test would be reliable because it yielded the same answers from people who had the same symptoms.

But reliability is not the only thing doctors need in the tools they use to make a diagnosis. Diagnostic tests also need specificity, which means that they have a high level of ability to identify one certain disease. If the test says you have strep, then 99 percent of the time, you do. Diagnostic tests also need sensitivity, meaning that if any of the bacteria are present, the test is sensitive enough to tell us so.

Then there is the issue of validity. In medicine, it means that when a test is positive for a disease, the patient definitely has the disease. The test results are valid and so is the diagnosis. In treating sore throats, the current standard of care for patients with pain on swallowing, fever, and a red throat is to do a rapid strep screen. If this test is positive, then the diagnosis of strep throat has a high reliability, specificity, and validity. If it is positive, you have strep because this is a very accurate test.

But suppose we said that all we needed to make a diagnosis of strep throat was a sore, red throat. If that was our standard for the diagnosis, we would diagnose a lot more patients with strep, but not all of them would have it. Our test, the red sore throat, would be reliable, meaning that every time I saw a red throat, I would call it strep. But it would not be valid—that is, it would

---

[13]Horwitz, *The Loss of Sadness*, 117, 118, 120.

not be correct, because some, if not most, red throats are caused by viruses, not strep.

Lab tests are the tools that allow medicine to make valid diagnoses. As Horwitz noted, if cough were the only criteria for tuberculosis, then lots of people could be reliably diagnosed with TB, but the results would not be valid.[14] The chest x-ray, TB skin test, and other tests decide which coughs are viral and which ones indicate TB.

This explains the problem with diagnoses of depression made using the criteria from the DSM-3 and all subsequent revisions. The criteria can reliably identify people who answer the diagnostic questions a certain way as having the symptoms of depression. However, I and others would argue that the diagnosis is not valid. It labels more people with depression than actually have it, because it lacks the testing ability to confirm the presence of a disease. The DSM criteria do not distinguish between symptoms of sadness due to identifiable causes and sadness that has no cause the patient can describe. Nothing in the criteria can tell the physician or the psychiatrist if Susan was stricken with depression out of the clear blue sky (disordered sadness) or if she lost her job three weeks ago and just had her house repossessed (normal sadness).

It is this lack of validity that Horwitz and others say leads to an overdiagnosis of depression by anyone who uses the DSM criteria (and any self-rating scale or survey based on them). It is possible that 90 percent of those diagnosed with depression today may be just like Susan.[15] They suffer sadness and it affects their whole lives. But they suffer that sadness because they lost something precious that they are not likely to get back.

---

[14]Horwitz, *The Loss of Sadness*, 151.

[15]Jerome Wakefield, Mark Schmitz, Michael First, Allan Horwitz, "Extending the Bereavement Exclusion for Major Depression to Other Losses," *Archives of General Psychiatry,* vol. 64 (April 2007) 438. "The results have substantial implications for MDD (Major Depressive Disorder) diagnosis, especially inasmuch as bereavement or some other loss reportedly precedes more than 90% of index episodes in MDD cases . . . ."

Normal Sadness—Biologically Designed?

If our only response is that their sadness is the disease of depression, it will affect the way we look at their problem and the things we do to try to help. Let's say that a woman comes to my office because she is anxious and depressed. She believes she has a disease—depression. Then she tells me that the man she had been living with for the last ten years has left her to raise their three children alone. It is obvious that she really does have something to worry about and good reason to be sad.

Her boyfriend left a month ago and she is still worried and sad, so she meets the basic DSM criteria for a depression diagnosis: Her sadness has gone on for two weeks. She is not eating because she has no appetite. She has no interest in doing things she once considered enjoyable. She cannot sleep or concentrate on her work. She certainly has no interest in men. Her reason for making an appointment with me is to get a prescription for the same medicine her girlfriend takes. The girlfriend told her it would help her get over the loss of her boyfriend.

Most people today would view the pain this woman is suffering as useless. The best thing we can do for her is to relieve that pain. But Horwitz and Wakefield would disagree. Not only would they say she is not depressed, they would say her sadness is a "biologically designed," useful part of her being. They call it a "normal part of human nature."[16]

The authors offer support for this argument that sadness is "a result of human species-typical biological design" in the important functions it serves.[17] Normal sadness draws social support to the sufferer. When a man loses his job, his real friends will find him in order to help and encourage. The widow generally will be surrounded by those who care for her.[18]

---

[16]Horwitz, *The Loss of Sadness*, 43.
[17]Ibid., 55.
[18]Ibid., 67. Disordered sadness or depression may not bring the same kind of help or consideration. It is noted that people who are depressed without cause for prolonged periods often drive friends away.

Normal sadness may also serve a protective function by limiting our losses. There are times when continuing to fight may only result in further harm, so sadness and the lack of energy that goes with it have a useful purpose. The man who leaves his job in a dispute because he does not have the will to fight may avoid the pain of hanging around to be fired.[19]

A third aspect of normal sadness that Horwitz and Wakefield offer as proof of its biological design is the human tendency to quit doing things that are failing. When failure causes us to be significantly sad, we are likely to quit investing our time and emotional energy in it. The woman who spends months working in an office where she is constantly criticized and has no real friends may decide that the job is not worth the daily sadness. If the company downsizes and she is offered the choice to leave or to compete for another job, her sadness may "protect" her from choosing to stay.[20]

I believe that Horwitz and Wakefield are correct in their view that sadness is a necessary and useful part of our being. I believe that it is an important aspect of the way God created us. If it is, then we have a legitimate option to approach suffering and sadness differently, and this will benefit people like Susan. Instead of seeing the normal sadness that accompanies illness and loss as a disease, Susan might see it as valuable part of her being. Susan's physical pain is what led her to see her doctor; at some point this could result in a diagnosis and cure. The emotional sadness that came with it brought the support of her loved ones. Eventually, she gave up trying to escape her sadness with medicine that brought little comfort but had significant side effects. In the end, it led her to look somewhere else for help. There are parallels to the three aspects of biologically designed sadness that Horwitz and Wakefield describe.

If the estimate is correct and 90 percent[21] of those diagnosed with depression are simply sad because of a significant loss, it may also

---

[19]Horwitz, *The Loss of Sadness*, 68. This is a behavior seen in male animals, such as wolves, who fight for territory and mates. The wolf who is about to lose and be killed will roll over on his back and expose his neck, signaling to the other wolf that he surrenders. The surrendering wolf must leave, but will live. The wolf who continues the fight may die.

[20]Ibid., 69.

[21]Wakefield, "Extending Bereavement Exclusion . . . " 438.

be true that they are the nearly 90 percent of patients for whom current medication is no more effective than a placebo.[22] Then what more is there to offer them? Irving Kirsch would say that talking with someone or conversational therapy would help them cope with their sadness.[23] And on this point, Kirsch is mostly correct.

God the Designer and His Goals

Nearly two thousand years ago, the apostle Paul stood in Athens and spoke before Greeks who were the most educated people of their day. As pagans they worshiped all kinds of gods, and one of those gods gave Paul the opportunity to introduce his hearers to the true God and his Son, Jesus Christ. Paul noticed that one of the altars on Mars Hill was dedicated to the unknown god (Acts 17:16–34). The Greeks did not wish to omit any deity deserving worship, so they worshiped the one they did not know—just in case. Paul told them who that unknown God was; some believed and some mocked.

Horwitz says that sadness is a biological design we may need. Paul identifies the unknown "designer" and, in another letter, he reflects on the need we sometimes have for sadness.

For though I caused you sorrow by my letter, I do not regret it; though I did regret it—for I see that that letter caused you sorrow, though only for a while—I now rejoice, not that you were made sorrowful, but that you were made sorrowful to the point of repentance; for you were made sorrowful according to the will of God, so that you might not suffer loss in anything through us. For the sorrow that is according to the will of God produces a repentance without regret, leading to salvation, but the sorrow of the world produces death. For behold what earnestness this very thing, this godly sorrow, has produced in you: what vindication of yourselves, what indignation, what fear, what longing, what zeal, what avenging of wrong! In everything you demonstrated yourselves to be innocent in the matter.

—2 Corinthians 7:8–11

[22]Begley, "Antidepressants Do/Don't Work," 38.
[23]Irving Kirsch, The Emperor's New Drugs, 158.

According to Paul, sorrow or sadness can be very important to us and serves a useful purpose. Understanding this point could have changed Susan's life, not to mention the rest of us who are saddened by our problems. For Paul, sorrow that was according to the will of God was good because it led to repentance and salvation. The sorrow of the world, on the other hand, led to death.

The context of Paul's statement starts in the first letter he wrote to the Corinthians. In it, he demanded that the Corinthians deal with a young man who was involved in sexual sin with his father's wife. The church had been tolerating the young man's sin, allowing him to continue in fellowship with the church. Paul told them to cast the man out.

> I have decided to deliver such a one to Satan for the destruction of his flesh, so that his spirit may be saved in the day of the Lord Jesus . . . . REMOVE THE WICKED MAN FROM AMONG YOURSELVES.
> —1 Corinthians 5:5, 13

The Corinthian church responded by doing just that. This seems harsh by today's standards, but Paul had a specific goal in mind. He wanted the Corinthians to sorrow over the sin they had tolerated, and he wanted the man in question to sorrow over the sin he had committed. He wanted all of them to repent, and he says so in his second letter. For that reason, he was glad that he made them sorrow, because it drove them to repentance and to God.

In his second letter to the Corinthians, Paul also made it clear that the sorrow he caused them had one more goal. Since the man had repented, the Corinthian church was instructed to forgive him and take him back into fellowship. The sorrow and sadness in this case was intended to be part of the process that restored him to the church (2 Cor. 2:1–10). For Paul, there were two kinds of sorrow or sadness, similar in some ways to the Horwitz view. Instead of normal or disordered sadness, there was godly sorrow that led to repentance and worldly sorrow that led to death.

Sorrow and sadness are tools God uses to draw us to him. His intent is to change the direction and content of our lives. Jesus used Martha's great sadness over Lazarus's death to show her the glory of God. God used sorrow to rescue the Corinthian church and the young adulterer from their sins. In both cases, the end product was joy. Susan could have found that joy years earlier if she had understood pain and sadness in this way.

If Susan had known that God calls to us in our sorrow, she could have responded to her trouble differently. C. S. Lewis once observed that "God whispers to us in our pleasures, speaks in our conscience, but shouts in our pains; it is His megaphone to rouse a deaf world."[24] There is a certain sense of peace and hope that comes from understanding that, in the middle of our sorrow, God wants to talk to us. And, just as he did with Martha, Mary, and Lazarus, he wants us to know that he is aware of all our troubles, he cares intensely about us, he has a plan, and he is expecting that we will wonder why?

For the 90 percent of the depressed for whom trouble is the source of their sadness, this is good news. For the remaining 10 percent—and for everyone who struggles with depression for whatever cause—knowing that God cares can bring real hope.

I am often asked if I believe that the 10 percent with unexplained sadness represent a disease. The answer is: I don't know. Nor does anyone else. No one in medicine, psychology, or biblical counseling should surrender to the argument that prolonged, unexplained sadness is a disease. We should want a better explanation in just the same way that Paul Ehrlich and Robin Marshall looked for a better explanation for disease that they wanted to treat. Until we have a pathological explanation for the 10 percent, we should be willing to say "I don't know." And we should continue to offer hope, from the truth of Scripture, to those with sad moods.

In the chapters that follow, we will examine the different functions that sadness and sorrow can have in our lives. Instead of seeing sadness as depression in a medical disease model, we can see it for what God, the Designer, intended it to be.

---

[24]C. S. Lewis, *The Problem of Pain* (New York: Macmillan: 1944).

6

The Gift of Sadness

As I travel to teach about biblical counseling, I often comment that God gives parents gifts that can be hard to identify as such. When we need to learn patience, he sends us sons. And when we need compassion, he sends us daughters. In the same sense, sadness is a gift from God. It is sent into our lives to do things that can come to us in no other way.

In the Bible translation I use (New American Standard Bible), the English word "sadness" appears just once. The word "sad" is found twelve times and the word "sorrow" thirty-nine. "Sadness" makes its one appearance in Nehemiah 2. Nehemiah was in Susa because of the deportation of the Jews. He was a servant of King Artaxerxes.

News came to him one day that the walls of Jerusalem had been torn down and the gates of the city burned. The news had a profound effect on Nehemiah and changed his mood. As he carried out his duties as cupbearer, the change in Nehemiah's attitude and appearance was noticed by the king.

So the king said to me, "Why is your face sad though you are not sick? This is nothing but sadness of heart." Then I was very much afraid. I said to the king, "Let the king live forever. Why should my face not be sad when the city, the place of my fathers' tombs, lies desolate and its gates have been consumed by fire?" Then the king said to me, "What would you request?" So I prayed to the God of heaven. I said to the king, "If it please the king, and if your servant has found favor before you, send me to Judah, to the city of my fathers' tombs, that I may rebuild it."

—Nehemiah 2:2–5

Artaxerxes responded by giving Nehemiah permission to travel to Jerusalem and fix the walls, as well as the funds to do the work. That is the last time we read of Nehemiah's sad mood or facial expression. Nehemiah fits the pattern of "normal sadness." The king noted that he was not sick. His sad face and sadder heart were a direct result of personal loss. His home, Jerusalem, was in ruins. The extent of his sadness was proportionate to the size of the problem, which was big. His mood disturbance continued until it was solved. But without that gift of sadness, the rest of Nehemiah's story might never have occurred.

If we consider Horwitz's three purposes for normal sadness (including social support, giving up when continuing to fight would only cause more damage, and dropping out of failing efforts), it is the first and second purposes that seem to come into play for Nehemiah. The second can be seen in the way Nehemiah responds to the king's statement, "This is nothing but sadness of heart." Nehemiah was scared to death! I think he might have been tempted to tell Artaxerxes that he was sick, but to do so would have been a lie.

However, Nehemiah did tell his story. He took advantage of the opportunity to help his people. For whatever reason, Artaxerxes was drawn to his servant's heartfelt complaint. Nehemiah was no doubt a good worker and a good person, which may be why the king allowed himself to be drawn into the problem. Without a doubt, we can see God at work as Nehemiah prayed as fervently as Peter did when he was just about to sink under the waves. In any case, it is true that Nehemiah was sad and his king was drawn to that sadness in a helpful way.

Thus, in Nehemiah's case, it seems that sadness was a normal part of his being and it had a cause. It was useful to Nehemiah (and his people) as it drew the support of those around him. Nehemiah's sadness drove him directly to God in prayer, and it ended when a solution arrived. As we examine sadness or sorrow in the Bible, this is the pattern we will typically find.

If we are going to help people struggling with sadness that has been labeled as depression, we need to answer three questions. (1) Where does the sadness come from? (2) What benefit can come from it? (3) What can we do as Christians to bring it to a useful end? These questions apply particularly to the "depressed" among us who have an identifiable cause for their sadness.

Where Does the Sadness Come From?

If sadness is connected to loss, the history of normal sadness starts in the garden of Eden, the scene of humanity's greatest loss. Imagine making a decision that will wreck your finances for the next twenty years, right into what should have been your retirement on a beach. Then multiply the emotion you feel by a billion! Now you can begin to sense the crushing emotional weight Adam and Eve must have felt, standing outside the garden and knowing they would never get back inside.

They could see all the good things they had lost. Fear of God replaced the fellowship they had enjoyed. Pain would be a part of childbirth. Toil would be added to labor because the ground would grow thorns and thistles as quickly as grain. An angel with a flaming sword stood at the garden gate to prevent their return. An uncertain world awaited them into which the ultimate Enemy had been introduced. As Romans 5:12 summarizes, "Therefore, just as through one man sin entered into the world, and death through sin, and so death spread to all men, because all sinned."

Our capacity for sadness, joy, and other emotions is part of our created being. We were created in God's image and this includes the capacity for emotion. "Let Us make man in Our image, according to Our likeness." (Gen. 1:26). Remarkably, the first use of any word pertaining to sad, sadness, or sorrow appears in Genesis 6:6. There God said that he was "sorry" that he had created man because his every thought was continually evil. I do not believe it is any mere "biological design" or accident that we can feel sadness. It appears that God created us that way, in his image, and for good reason.

The wickedness of humankind "grieved" God so much that he said, "I am sorry that I have made them." His grief led to the judgment of the flood, which killed all except Noah, who "found favor in the eyes of the LORD" (Gen. 6:8). When men and women chose to sin, it resulted in God expressing sorrow. We too experience sorrow over the sinful choices others make. It has been this way since the Fall.

There are many biblical examples of loss-connected sadness to which we can relate. In Genesis 40, Joseph, and the king's butler and baker, were in prison. All had lost their freedom. The butler and baker had lost their jobs and status, and their futures were in doubt. They had dreams that seemed to be connected to their predicament but they could not understand them. Their sadness was appropriate in light of their problems. It drew Joseph's attention, who interpreted their dreams. Things ended well for the butler when he returned to work. Unfortunately, sadness ended abruptly for the baker when the king hanged him.

Hannah in the book of First Samuel is another example of sadness brought on by a serious problem. Hannah had been living for years in a home where her husband had another wife. The other woman had children and Hannah did not. As the years passed with no children born to her, Hannah's sadness grew. It affected her appearance, her marriage, and eventually her worship of God.

> Then Hannah rose after eating and drinking in Shiloh. Now Eli the priest was sitting on the seat by the doorpost of the temple of the LORD. She, greatly distressed, prayed to the LORD and wept bitterly. She made a vow and said, "O LORD of hosts, if You will indeed look on the affliction of Your maidservant and remember me, and not forget Your maidservant, but will give Your maidservant a son, then I will give him to the LORD all the days of his life, and a razor shall never come on his head."
>
> —1 Samuel 1:9–11

Hannah had been miserable for years as her husband's rival wife provoked her. When she appeared for worship that year, Eli the priest looked at her silently praying, with her lips moving, and at first assumed she was drunk. But then Eli heard her petition and prayed for her. God answered those prayers and Hannah conceived and gave birth to Samuel. The next time we see Hannah, she is a different person.

> Then Hannah prayed and said, "My heart exults in the LORD; my horn is exalted in the LORD, my mouth speaks boldly against my enemies, because I rejoice in Your salvation. There is no one holy like the LORD, indeed, there is no one besides You, nor is there any rock like our God."
>
> —1 Samuel 2:1–2

Her sad mood had a cause. It drew helpful attention from those around her. When the problem ended, so did her sadness. But in most clinical settings today, Hannah's sadness would be labeled as the disease of depression. There are many biblical examples of problem-induced sadness that would today be diagnosed as a mood disorder. But people who face financial loss or struggle with raising difficult children will suffer with normal sadness.

The children of Israel knew all about this kind of sadness. The exodus is an amazing story of salvation, redemption, and deliverance by God through ten of the most spectacular plagues in history. As they left Egypt, they walked with God, who led them as a cloud and protected them as a pillar of fire. As astounding as that history was, after they had been delivered from the slavery of Egypt and watched Pharaoh's army drown in the Red Sea, the Israelites nevertheless built a golden calf and worshiped it as god.

God's response was to tell Moses to stand back while he destroyed the nation and replaced it with Moses and his descendants. Moses intervened and offered to be blotted out of the Book of Life in place of the children of Israel, which God refused to do.

> The LORD said to Moses, "Whoever has sinned against Me, I will blot him out of My book. But go now, lead the people where I told you. Behold, My angel shall go before you; nevertheless in the day when I punish, I will punish them for their sin." Then the

LORD smote the people, because of what they did with the calf which Aaron had made.

Then the LORD spoke to Moses, "Depart, go up from here, you and the people whom you have brought up from the land of Egypt, to the land of which I swore to Abraham, Isaac, and Jacob, saying, 'To your descendants I will give it.' I will send an angel before you and I will drive out the Canaanite, the Amorite, the Hittite, the Perizzite, the Hivite and the Jebusite. Go up to a land flowing with milk and honey; for I will not go up in your midst, because you are an obstinate people, and I might destroy you on the way." When the people heard this sad word, they went into mourning, and none of them put on his ornaments.

—Exodus 32:33–33:3

The children of Israel made a sinful choice. Many of them died and God said that he would not travel to the Promised Land with the rest of them. They suffered a huge loss, similar in a way to the loss suffered by Adam and Eve. Their sin robbed them of God's presence and they mourned. I suspect that their sadness continued until, as a result of Moses' intercession on their behalf, God later stated that his presence would go with them into the new land. But the initial sadness was connected to the loss in its timing and severity.

Another aspect of normal sadness is the grief we experience when we lose friends or loved ones through death or their temporary or permanent departure. As we have seen, Mary and Martha experienced grief when Lazarus died. The loss was identifiable and their sadness was in proportion to the loss suffered. It attracted the attention of friends and brought support. It also brought real help, and this is where sadness as a creation of God meets God's provision for our need.

The interaction Jesus had with Martha, Mary, and Lazarus had four important elements. Throughout Lazarus's illness, death and resurrection, as God, Jesus knew all about the problem. Despite his apparent inaction, Jesus had a plan that would result in God's glory and Lazarus's good. When confronting Martha and Mary's heartache, Jesus cared and wept. Jesus listened without judgment or condemnation to their questions and heartfelt complaints.

God or Biological Design?

It is difficult to know exactly what Horwitz and Wakefield meant when they said that sadness is "biologically designed" because they make no attempt to explain the idea.[1] As Christians look at sadness in the light of Scripture, we see a sovereign God graciously at work on our behalf. We know that "all things were made by him," including our emotional responses to the ups and downs of life. It is no accident that when we suffer loss, we respond emotionally for a time and with an intensity that matches the problem. God made us that way in his image. We know he understands our sadness because he has experienced it, "having been tested in all points just as we are" (Heb. 4:14). As we struggle and suffer, we can be certain that Jesus knows.

When we compare Horwitz's concept of biological design to God as Creator, there is obviously a great advantage in having God as our designer. As certainly as we know that Jesus knew about Martha, Mary, and Lazarus, we can be certain that God cares and listens to us when we struggle. The Bible assures us that Jesus can "sympathize with our weakness" and that he was tested with the struggles we face. For that reason, we are told to ask for help.

Therefore let us draw near with confidence to the throne of grace, so that we may receive mercy and find grace to help in time of need.
—Hebrews 4:16

When we face trouble, we do not have to look at the devastation and shake our fist at a god who has no eyes or ears. God is listening; he cares, and he offers his gracious help to those who trust in him.

Throughout his Chronicles of Narnia, C. S. Lewis shows us characters like Lucy, who are thrown into great danger and adversity without a clue as to why. Along the way there are clues to tell them that Aslan is behind the scenes, working the situation toward his goal and their good, but this reality is not easily seen. Lucy often saw glimpses of Aslan, only to miss really seeing him and

---

[1] Horwitz, *The Loss of Sadness*, 55.

his purposes being fulfilled in the midst of—and through—the difficult circumstance.

When Horwitz says that sadness has a purpose, he does see a faint glimpse of the spiritual reality the Bible teaches. The truth we see clearly in Scripture is that Jesus had a plan for Lazarus's illness and for Martha and Mary's sadness. God used that pain, suffering, and emotional turmoil to fulfill a great purpose.

Within our hearts we know there is a purpose in our problems, because God planted that knowledge in us. It makes us look for him just as Lucy looked for Aslan. But what benefit comes from sadness? In the next chapter we will examine the second question we need to face as Christians who suffer or who want to help others who suffer.

7

What Good Is Sadness?

Like the word "sadness," the word "depression" does not appear often in the Bible. Depending on the translation, it may not appear at all. In the King James Version and the New International Version it is nowhere to be found. In the New American Standard version it appears twice. In 2 Samuel 3:14 the Hebrew word *dal* can be translated as low, weak, poor, or thin and from that it would be hard to decide if Amnon could meet today's criteria for depression.

In 2 Corinthians 7:6 Paul speaks of himself when he said, "But God who comforts the depressed comforted us by the coming of Titus." It is possible, but not likely, that Paul met the DSM criteria for depression, I doubt that the word used was meant to tell us that Paul had a medical illness. I suspect it simply meant that Paul was discouraged by his circumstances. How can a word so important in our day be nearly absent from most translations of Scripture? Why would no one in 1611 use the word when the King James Version was translated?

There are two reasonable explanations for the absence of the word "depression." Five hundred years ago when people suffered and sorrowed, they didn't think of it in terms of a disease; they called it sadness or sorrow. But when our culture encounters sadness, it sees depression.

One recent paraphrase of the Bible applies the word "depressed" to Hannah, illustrating the change in the way we see and talk about sadness.[1] If you add that to our strong societal bias to see depression as a biological disease, this raises several important questions. What possible good is it for someone to live in a state of sadness? What good did it do Hannah? We want to answer that question because we want to know what good sadness will do for us.

So much of life today seems to depend on feeling good. If I'm not happy or things are not going well, I can turn on the television and watch five minutes of commercials every twelve minutes that will tell me what I need to escape sadness and find fulfillment. But for most of us, the answers in the commercials do not seem to be working.

I suspect that sadness is something we all want to avoid, not something we see as an opportunity. Most of us would run from the chance to suffer and I know I have done my share of running. But it might change the direction we run if we understood just how much a part of God's creation sadness is. In his book *Smooth Stones*, Joe Coffey reflects on the truth that God created us with the unmistakable imprint of his design.

Coffey writes that astrophysicist Brandon Carter published a paper in 1973 in which he asserted that the world had been designed for just one purpose, and that was for human beings to live here. He called it the Anthropic principle.[2] Carter believed that the complex nature of all the ingredients and events that had to be in place for human beings to live on earth could only mean that there was a designer behind it. Any small change in the ingredients or the process would have resulted in a planet like Mars—almost right, but completely uninhabitable. Every detail was important. When Christians see that, we see the hand of God at work.

I would assert that sadness is just as much a part of God's carefully designed creation as the air we breathe and the water we drink. It is

---

[1] *The Message*, 1 Samuel 1 (Colorado Springs, CO.: Navpress, 2002).
[2] Joe Coffey, *Smooth Stones* (Adelphi, Md.: Cruciform Press, 2011), 41.

just as important to us as the distance we sit from the sun and the time it takes the earth to rotate. When Paul speaks of this aspect of sorrow he says, "For the sorrow that is according to the will of God produces a repentance without regret, leading to salvation, but the sorrow of the world produces death" (2 Cor. 7:10). Sorrow according to the will of God is a tool he uses to lead us to salvation. There are all kinds of vitally important aspects of our existence, but none is more important than our salvation.

This gives us the opportunity to look at sadness in a completely different light. Instead of running from it, we can stop to see it for what it is—a tool God will use to speak to us if we are willing to listen. With these ideas in mind, Hannah and Paul are good examples of the different ways God uses sadness to accomplish his work in our lives.

Where Are You When I Need You?

Hannah's sadness drew the attention of those around her and gained her the support of her husband, just as Horwitz said it should. But that is about as much help as Hannah received from those around her. It did not bring any relief from the taunting of her husband's other wife, nor did it result in children. From a secular psychological or sociological viewpoint, the benefit Hannah received from her natural response to adversity wasn't much. So, if we are going to say that sadness is valuable and suffering is a benefit for us as Christians, what do we see in her story that tells us that the struggle is worth it?

Looking for the answer to the "What good is it?" question leads us directly to the "Where were you when I needed you?" question. This question usually arises when we face problems that make us sad. The answer for Hannah was that God was always there. In the same way that Jesus knew about Lazarus, God knew all about Hannah's childlessness. The account says twice that it was God who closed her womb. He not only knew about Hannah's trouble, it was part of his plan for her life.

Just as Jesus had a plan that would result in God's glory and Lazarus's good, God had a plan for Hannah. We may never know exactly what it was, but it is safe to say that Hannah's suffering drove her to God. She was stuck in a situation for which there was no human solution. Year after year, the constant in her life was that trip to Shiloh, where she would present her problem to God with tears.

If sadness turns our hearts toward God, this is an enormous benefit to all of us. Few things in life bring greater emotional turmoil than illness. It is even worse when we face death. My brother once told me that when his doctor said he had a skin cancer, he didn't hear another word the man said. He was certain that the doctor must have had something else important to tell him, but he missed it all. Instead he was immediately pulled into an emotional whirlpool that threatened to drag him under.

In the years I have practiced medicine, I have watched this happen when I have had the sad duty of telling patients that they have a serious illness. I know I must find a way to give them hope during the short time I have with them or they will drown. By driving us towards God, sadness drives us to hope. The psalmist said it very well.

I love the LORD, because He hears
My voice and my supplications.
Because He has inclined His ear to me,
Therefore I shall call upon Him as long as I live.
The cords of death encompassed me
And the terrors of Sheol came upon me;
I found distress and sorrow.
Then I called upon the name of the LORD:
"O LORD, I beseech You, save my life!"

Gracious is the LORD, and righteous;
Yes, our God is compassionate.
The LORD preserves the simple;
I was brought low, and He saved me.
—Psalm 116:1–6

Again, we see that when we encounter trouble, God is always there listening. As long as we live and want to talk, God is bending his ear in our direction. Any day, any time, God is available, and willing, to listen to his children. The only limit we see is our willingness to talk. Another psalm says, "There is not a word in my tongue, but, lo, O LORD, thou knowest it altogether" (Ps. 139:4, KJV). He is not like an answering machine with ten options but no live person to hear you! God is listening. What a comfort that is to those who sorrow without a friend to hear and help.

The psalmist says that something as serious as death or illness brings sorrow. The next thing that happens is that he calls upon the name of the Lord. Just as we would expect, the normal God-given response to trouble and the sorrow it brings is for us to turn to God for help. The writer cries out, "I beg You, save my life!" Just like Peter as he sank beneath the waves, we are made to cry out to God, "Lord, if you don't save me, nobody will!"

In the process, we see the character of God. He is gracious, righteous, and compassionate in his response to our prayers. He doesn't answer our prayers based on how smart we are. Instead, the Psalm says he preserves those who are simple. When God hears our prayers, it means that help is coming. He heard me and he saved me. And that help will be better than any solution to our trouble we could have thought of or hoped for.

Trouble and Sadness: First Signs That Help Is Coming!

An important aspect of trouble and sorrow is that they can be one of the first signs that help is coming. Paul's transformation from being a man who hated Christians to a missionary for the faith was accomplished through amazing adversity. We first meet Paul (known as Saul at the time) holding the coats of those who are stoning Stephen (Acts 7:58). At that point, Saul was a respected, self-assured, religiously approved Pharisee of Pharisees. Watching Stephen beaten to death with large stones ignited a passion in him for killing Christians. He became famous for it. At the time of his conversion, he was on his way to Damascus with the official paperwork to arrest and murder more Christians. He was the point man for the persecution of the church.

For those of us who read Paul's New Testament letters, it is hard to imagine just how vicious Saul was until God dropped a huge problem into his life.

> As he was traveling, it happened that he was approaching Damascus, and suddenly a light from heaven flashed around him; and he fell to the ground and heard a voice saying to him, "Saul, Saul, why are you persecuting Me?" And he said, "Who are You, Lord?" And He said, "I am Jesus whom you are persecuting, but get up and enter the city, and it will be told you what you must do." The men who traveled with him stood speechless, hearing the voice but seeing no one. Saul got up from the ground, and though his eyes were open, he could see nothing; and leading him by the hand, they brought him into Damascus. And he was three days without sight, and neither ate nor drank.
>
> —Acts 9:3–9

In one stroke Jesus accomplishes several things. He stops Saul's persecution of the church, he reveals himself as God to Saul, and he opens the door for us to see the nature of grace. He lets Saul see enough of his glory that it blinds him. For all Saul knew that day, he would be blind for the rest of his life.

What a gift that blindness was! For three days he sat in the dark without eating or drinking. There was absolutely nothing to distract him from thinking about what he had been, what he had lost, and what he had ahead of him. There was nothing left to focus on but that bright, vivid impression of the face of Jesus and the faces of those he had persecuted and murdered. It was a gift.

Saul's suffering was an enormous gift. God could have simply dealt with him the same way he dealt with Herod and killed him. Instead God gave Saul grace. For the next three days, Saul prayed. Imagine the regret, the shame, the embarrassment and, yes, the sadness in which Saul was enveloped in his darkness. It drove him to God and his grace.

Hannah and Saul suffered for very different reasons. We would say that Hannah's problem was not caused by any action on her part. Saul, on the other hand, could draw a straight line between his behavior and his problem. But the end result was the same. The problem and the emotional turmoil drove them both to God. Many of us could tell similar stories of how sadness, suffering, and the problems of life drove us to God. For that reason, sadness as a created part of our being deserves to be valued.

Sadness and Suffering Drive Us to Grace

Hannah's suffering also made her a recipient of grace. Grace simply defined means "unmerited favor": I do not deserve and have not earned whatever it is I receive. Whatever I receive is a gift. Paul used Abraham to explain it.

> For if Abraham was justified by works, he has something to boast about, but not before God. For what does the Scripture say? "ABRAHAM BELIEVED GOD, AND IT WAS CREDITED TO HIM AS RIGHTEOUSNESS." . . . For this reason it is by faith, in order that it may be in accordance with grace, so that the promise will be guaranteed to all the descendants, not only to those who are of the Law, but also to those who are of the faith of Abraham, who is the father of us all . . .
>
> —Romans 4:2–3, 16

Not long ago, I was visiting my cousins in southern California and went to church with them. The sermon "happened" to be about Hannah and the problems we suffer. I left that morning with two things written in the margin of the bulletin. The pastor said, "Problems never come without purpose" and Hannah's name in Hebrew means "grace."[3]

I don't believe it was an accident that the pastor preached about Hannah on a day when I had traveled 2000 miles to be there and when I needed to hear about problems, sadness, and grace. I also don't believe it was an accident that Hannah's name means "grace." In truth, that is what her story is all about.

---

[3]"The Story of Hannah," sermon on 7/24/2011 by Dr. Stan Van Den Berg, Pastor, Covenant Presbyterian Church.

If you read the account quickly, you may think that this is a story about the evils of polygamy or the burden of infertility. And you would miss the point. It reflects the definition of womanhood in that era, when Rachel would tell Jacob to "give me children or I will die." Rachel and Hannah shared the view that they could not be complete as women unless they had sons.

If you are not careful, you might think that the point of the story is that God miraculously opened Hannah's womb to give her children. But the real point is how God worked in the heart of a woman whose sole desire was to have children. Hannah's situation truly was a burden and a heartache. But in the midst of it, Hannah was fixated on herself and her problem. It is there that we see God's grace at work.

Sadness Opens the Door to Change

From the time we see her in tears until she weans little Samuel and presents him at the temple for service to the Lord and Eli, Hannah changes. She changes from a sad woman who could only be fulfilled by having a child to a joyful woman who could give the person she valued most to the Lord. She did not go grudgingly to the temple with her son Samuel; she went with joy to leave behind part of her heart.

> Then Hannah prayed and said,
> "My heart exults in the LORD;
> My horn is exalted in the LORD,
> My mouth speaks boldly against my enemies,
> Because I rejoice in Your salvation.
> There is no one holy like the LORD,
> Indeed, there is no one besides You,
> Nor is there any rock like our God."
> —1 Samuel 2:1–2

The rest of Hannah's prayer is a testimony to God's sovereign grace. The remarkable thing about it is that God could send a problem into Hannah's life that brought her sadness, and then allow that sadness to drive her to himself, to grace, and to change. If we could do away with all suffering and sadness, we would indeed suffer a great loss. The real importance of sadness is that it drives us to the only place and power that bring about real change in our lives.

In the New Testament, Paul was an example of God's gracious, redemptive purposes behind suffering and sadness for the believer. When Jesus sent Ananias to retrieve and heal Paul, the Lord told Ananias that he must show Paul how much he would suffer for Christ. Paul's own testimony was that he had suffered much.

> . . . far more imprisonments, beaten times without number, often in danger of death. Five times I received from the Jews thirty-nine lashes. Three times I was beaten with rods, once I was stoned, three times I was shipwrecked, a night and a day I have spent in the deep. I have been on frequent journeys, in dangers from rivers, dangers from robbers, dangers from my countrymen, dangers from the Gentiles, dangers in the city, dangers in the wilderness, dangers on the sea, dangers among false brethren; I have been in labor and hardship, through many sleepless nights, in hunger and thirst, often without food, in cold and exposure.
>
> —2 Corinthians 11:23–27

Few American believers have suffered physically the way Paul did for his faith. Paul's response to his loss was, "I count all things to be loss in view of the surpassing value of knowing Christ Jesus my Lord, for whom I have suffered the loss of all things, and count them but rubbish so that I may gain Christ, and may be found in Him . . ." (Phil. 3:8–9a).

When we first meet Saul, the thing he valued most in life was his religion. He was a Pharisee of Pharisees and proud of it. He was willing to kill anyone who threatened his prized religion. Yet Paul becomes the living example of grace, and the reality is that the adversity he faced was part of that grace. Saul went from being an enforcer for a religion of works to being Paul, the living, breathing example of salvation by grace. Saul went from being an enforcer for a religion of works to being Paul, the living, breathing, example of salvation by grace, and he would boldly proclaim that he was saved by "grace . . . through faith; and that not of [our]selves, it is the gift of God" (Eph. 2:8). Instead of working to earn God's acceptance, Paul became God's workmanship.

Paul looked at suffering and sadness and called it a "momentary, light affliction" that would produce "for us an eternal weight of glory far beyond all comparison" (2 Cor. 4:17). Most of the world sees sadness as a non-productive inconvenience at best. Very few of us believe, like Horwitz, that it has any real value. Instead, we count up workdays, doctor visits, and the cost of medicine and reckon the loss to be in the billions. Paul viewed sadness and suffering as the means God used to grow him in grace.

Sadness Opens the Door to Repentance and . . .

There are many other things that sadness or sorrow can bring into our lives that make it worth enduring. Repentance is one of them. Repentance is a biblical idea that means "to change your mind" or "to turn around and head the other way." For the Christian, sadness or sorrow that leads to repentance is a great gift.

It certainly was for the young man in Corinth who repented of his adultery. It was also a great gift for the church there as it repented of the careless attitude toward the sin within their congregation. Paul said that this godly sorrow produced in them a real earnestness for the faith.

Times of sadness can bring reconciliation between loved ones. My brother, a pastor, says that whenever he preaches at a funeral, he always takes time to urge those present to consider reconciling with those from whom they are estranged. He says it generally works well. The finality of death reminds us that there will not always be time to say the words that need to be said to settle old arguments. The sadness we feel in losing friends and loved ones can soften our hearts towards those who remain.

Sadness Equips Us for Service

There are many other good things that sadness can drive us to do, but I will end with this last important one. Suffering and struggle equip us to help those who will face the same kinds of problems.

Paul knew this because he suffered. And so he said, "Blessed be the God and Father of our Lord Jesus Christ, the Father of mercies and God of all comfort; who comforts us in all our affliction so that we will be able to comfort those who are in any affliction with the comfort with which we ourselves are comforted by God" (2 Cor. 1:3–4).

When we struggle in life, it equips us to help others who will face the same problems. When you understand that God leaves us here on earth to serve him by serving others, then sadness becomes vocational training for the believer. As I write this chapter, I have looked at my Tweet deck to see what the rest of the world is doing. I have been amazed at the number of people I know who are struggling on this particular day. Some have lost work, others are dealing with chronic pain, and some are burdened by the daily cares of life. But as we struggle, all of us are preparing for a time when we will be able to say to another brother or sister in Christ, "I have been there and here is how God graciously took me through it."

All of our tears and sighs are to be studied for the benefit of others. One "tweeter" quoted Peter who said, "If when you do what is right and suffer for it you patiently endure it, this finds favor with God. For you have been called for this purpose, since Christ also suffered for you, leaving you an example for you to follow in His steps" (1 Peter 2:20–21). The ultimate confirmation that suffering and sadness are useful is our Savior's willingness to suffer for us. If Jesus suffered for us, we should be willing to do the same for others because we love him.

The interesting thing about the blizzard of tweets on suffering I read today was that it all started with a "random" quote from C. S. Lewis sent out by a site that daily sends out a 140-character-or-less quote. Today's quote was, "We're not necessarily doubting that God will do the best for us; we're wondering how painful the best will turn out to be."[4] This is at the heart of the question we considered in chapter 4. Though it is probably not possible to medically banish sadness from life, should we want to do so anyway?

---

[4] C. S. Lewis, *Letters of C. S. Lewis* (April 29, 1959) www.lanciaesmith.com (5/23/12).

I would say that the answer is an emphatic no based on what we have seen in Scripture. We cannot get rid of something God has created and intends to use in our lives for his glory and our good. The reason we ask the question is because, as Lewis said, we wonder how much pain there is going to be—and we really don't want to suffer it. It is not that we don't want to grow and change and become more like Christ. It's just that we have a normal aversion to painful things.

Sorrow, sadness, and the problems that bring them into our lives are important to our spiritual growth. In another quote, Lewis explains the struggle.

> Imagine yourself as a living house. God comes in to rebuild that house. At first, perhaps, you can understand what he is doing . . . But presently He starts knocking the house about in a way that hurts abominably and does not seem to make any sense. What on earth is He up to? The explanation is that He is building quite a different house from the one you thought. . . . You thought you were being made into a decent little cottage: but He is building a palace. He intends to come and live in it Himself.[5]

That is why we need the God-given ability to be sad. Sorrow, like happiness, is a normal part of our God-given emotions and he uses them in our spiritual growth.

To this point we have challenged many of the ideas used to explain mood disorders like depression. We have seen that it is not true that all unexplained medical symptoms and pain are the result of depression. We have seen that the diagnosis of depression is often made by physicians and others in health care without using the DSM criteria that are meant to define it. Furthermore, those criteria may not be able to make a valid diagnosis in as many as 90 percent of the patients it labels. Even more important, we have found that sadness is a useful part of our being, a gift from God meant for our good and his glory.

---

[5] C. S. Lewis, *Mere Christianity*. http://cslewiswisdom.blogspot.com/2011/08/imagine-yourself-living-house.html (5/23/2012).

There is one more area that deserves a challenge. Currently in medicine and counseling, it is assumed that once you have depression, you have a 50 to 70 percent chance of having it return even if you are successfully treated.[6] And since most practitioners believe that depression is usually a medical problem, they would say that the only reasonable way to escape it will be through medication. Here again, there are those who disagree even though they would not use the Bible to support their viewpoint. In the next chapter we will hear from them as we seek a response to the sadness that comes with the problems of life.

---

[6]WebMD, "Quitting therapy too soon," www.webmd.com (10/10/2011). "Quitting therapy too soon . . . can increase the risk your depression will come back. Sixty percent of people who have been depressed once will get depression again. Seventy percent of people who have been depressed twice will become depressed a third time. Sticking with treatment is the best way to prevent this from happening again or controlling a relapse before it becomes serious." Calculated out, this website would tell us that four out of ten will deal with depression at least on and off indefinitely.

8

Joy in the Mourning

When I graduated from medical school in 1975, no one pretended to know exactly why people became depressed. We knew there were lots of people like Susan who would struggle with sadness, but most of them seemed to have a good reason for it. Depressed people seemed to lead depressing lives; with Susan, the issue was her pain. Beyond that we had few answers.

Today people like Susan have the same kinds of problems. But instead of living in sad isolation wondering why, today they encounter people who are certain they understand the cause and cure for their dark moods. If the decade of seventies brought us the "Age of Aquarius" and the eighties gave us disco fever, we may look back at the last twenty years and call it the Age of Depression.

It's not hard to understand how so many people like Susan were diagnosed with depression, given the problems built into the DSM criteria. But that does not answer the question of why we feel the need to morph sadness into depression and treat it as a medical condition. Beyond that, why do we seem to be pressured to believe that depression is a permanent state?

When I think of Hannah and her problems, I have little doubt that she would have suffered more today than she did in her own time. If she were transported into our world of chemical imbalances, it is likely that she would have been labeled as depressed. It would be just as likely that she would be treated with one of our many medications. Statistically, there is nothing to say that she would have done better, and a growing conviction that she would have fared worse.

The reason we "need" to make sadness into a disease and the reason Hannah would have not done well today are one and the same. As a society, we have lost our understanding of the answers that worked so well for Hannah. We want and need an explanation when we feel bad and hope for relief. But we have forgotten the old remedy and so we need another.

Several changes have had a profound effect on the way Americans look at life. They would change the way Hannah might expect to be helped if she were today's thirty-something woman struggling with infertility, worry, and depression. Hannah struggled for years and brought her complaint to God in prayer. It was the obvious choice for Hannah but few would consider it today.

The reason people no longer turn first to their Bible, prayer, or their pastor for help is simple. Generally, people don't think as much about Christianity as they did fifty to one hundred years ago. Our nation has "progressed" beyond the narrow confines of the Christian faith.

From the City Set on a Hill to the Secular City

In my lifetime I have watched our nation move from John Winthrop's Puritan vision of "the city set on a hill" to the secular city. The process began in earnest in 1948 when the U. S. Supreme Court declared religious education in public schools to be unconstitutional. Other writers have detailed the sad history of our nation's gradual but steady departure from all things Christian. It is enough to say here that the majority of Americans no longer believe in absolute truth as revealed in the Bible.

This is most clearly seen among those born after 1960. The trend has come to be known as post-modernism.[1] The basic tenet of this philosophy is that my opinion or "truth" is just as valid as yours and you have no right to impose yours on me. "True for you, but not true for me," results in no clear narrative that objectively decides right and wrong.[2] The result is that, morally, Americans are doing "what was right in their own eyes" (see Judges 21:25). The Bible that was the foundation for law back in John Winthrop's day in 1630 no longer matters.

This has had devastating results in every aspect of life, including marriage, family, childhood, business, and government. Divorce, unmarried live-in couples, teenage pregnancy, sexually transmitted disease, general crime rates, corruption in government, and child pornography are just a few of the problems that have exploded in the last four decades.

Changing Morals and Immoral Choices Bring Pain

This change in perspective has been the source of our moral decline. It has also been very influential in the way we deal with problem behavior. The choice to live as we please often increases the worry, fear, and sadness we face. A good example of this reality is the common choice couples make to live together while unmarried. There are lots of reasons given for doing something that the Bible clearly describes as sexual sin. They include things like saving money on living expenses and the desire to avoid making a mistake by marrying someone they eventually might not love.

Couples who cohabit want the benefits of a domestic partnership without the legal entanglement. Some may believe that it will be easier to part ways should the time come when the "partnership" no longer meets their needs. The problem is that living with someone as if you are married will result in the same emotional,

---

[1]Drew Dyck, *Generation Ex-Christian: Why Young Adults Are Leaving the Faith and How to Bring Them Back* (Chicago: Moody Press, 2010), 21. This is an excellent description of how post-modern thinking has affected moral choices in the United States in the last forty years.
[2]Ibid., 21.

physical, and spiritual one-flesh connection that you have when actually married.[3]

I remember one patient who came to see me because he was struggling with a terribly depressed mood. When we talked through its history, I learned that it started when his girlfriend decided to move out and take their children with her after seven years of living together. The idea that he would suffer less because they weren't married was a sad myth. He struggled with anger, fear, worry, rejection, and a depressed mood just like a man who had just received his divorce papers and gone home to find the furniture gone.

The connection this man had with his "partner" was so tightly woven that it ripped his heart as she tore away from him. The mistake he made is a common one today. To think that we can live any way we choose and feel good about it is simply not true. The truth is that when we choose to sin, we suffer. The writer of Proverbs put it well when he said, "He who conceals his transgressions will not prosper. But he who confesses and forsakes them will find compassion" (Prov. 28:13).

It makes no difference if we choose to pretend that God does not exist or to think that the Bible's definitions of right and wrong do not apply to our modern age. When we choose to do wrong, we will suffer the consequences. Paul said it best in his letter to the Galatians. "Do not be deceived, God is not mocked; for whatever a man sows, this he will also reap. For the one who sows to his own flesh will from the flesh reap corruption, but the one who sows to the Spirit will from the Spirit reap eternal life" (Gal. 6:7–8).

The result is that when we choose to do wrong, we bear the emotional consequences. For that reason we "need" society to turn our emotional struggles into something that has nothing to do with our own behavior. It is more convenient to turn our sadness into depression than it is to repent.

---

[3]Genesis 2:24 and 1Corinthians 6:16 describe the binding nature of a sexual partnership.

Changing Moral Patterns Hurt Others

At the same time that many people are making moral and religious choices that hurt them, they also hurt others with those choices. When people choose to abandon God and his Word as their guide to life, they will inevitably hurt innocent bystanders. We rarely live alone on islands, and we cannot sin in a vacuum.

Hannah would make a fair example. She did not choose childlessness or the persecution that came with it. She would be like many men and women who suffer significant harm and loss at the hands of others. The problem today is that our new moral framework offers no help for their sorrow until it lasts more than two weeks—when it becomes depression.

Today's Hannah may be "liberated" from all kinds of "superstitious" biblical restrictions but she is just as interested in relief as the Hannah of Old Testament times. The difference is that she has been robbed of a biblical answer to deal with her suffering.

Willful Choices or Inherited Compulsions?

In the same way that our society's changing view of God and the Bible has been a force behind the desire to change sorrow into depression, it is also the drive behind the need to say that our emotions are beyond our control.

Worry, fear, anger, and sadness all have biblical definitions and remedies. The further we have gone from our biblical heritage, the more difficult it has become to deal with our negative emotions. At the same time, there has been an effort to redefine the causes of these emotions in order to ultimately reduce our responsibility for them.

While Robert Spitzer (unknowingly) lessened the validity of the DSM diagnosis of depression by ignoring issues of cause, others in psychiatric and genetic medicine were working with a very different idea. They believed that the reason people became depressed had less to do with their life experiences and more to do with their genes.

They believed that defects in our DNA could account for the as-yet-unproven "chemical imbalance" believed to be the cause of most emotional and behavioral disorders. Someone with a genetic defect was not responsible for it and could do nothing about it. The slogan was, "Depression is a flaw in chemistry, not character."[4]

This left people like Susan with two options. First, they could struggle with their emotions with little hope for change and tell themselves that it was a part of life, like gray hair and wrinkles. Or second, they could continue to look for medication that could compensate for the defective gene. These would be their only options if they believed that all depression is genetic. Fortunately, not everyone believes this.

Born to Be Depressed?

"Neurogenetic determinism" is a real mouthful. The term was coined in 1995 by Steven Rose to describe the theory that depression and other emotional and behavioral problems are caused by a disorder of our genetic material.[5] Those who hold to this concept would say that Hannah was depressed because she was born to be that way. The DNA her parents gave her caused her to respond to her life losses with a dark mood.

They would say that even if things got better and Hannah's circumstances changed, she would eventually settle back into depression. It was her set point and her destiny. Hannah could not change because her brain could not change.

But this view of human genetics and behavior is wrong, because Hannah did change. And Rose and other researchers have taken exception to the idea that things as complex as human behavior and emotion can always be explained by a defect in a single gene. While there are well-known diseases, such as Huntington's chorea, that are the result of single genetic defect, problems such as depression, worry, and anger are the product of multiple parts of our brains and bodies, thus requiring the input of many genes. Those behaviors arise from the interactions between who we are and our daily living experiences. Rose disagreed with the idea that

---

[4]Horwitz, *The Loss of Sadness.* This quote appears on the book cover.
[5]Steven Rose, "The Rise of Neurogenetic Determinism," *Nature*, vol. 373 (February 2, 1995), 380.

our emotions and behavior could be reduced to a simple connection between the problem gene and the behavior.[6]

I Can't Change My Genes!

Hannah's life was difficult and her profound change involved the providential action of God. Skeptics might dismiss Hannah, as some scientists do the virgin birth or resurrection. But to do so would be shortsighted. There are other people in really difficult situations who also change.

Few psychiatric problems are as difficult to deal with as Obsessive Compulsive Disorder. People with this diagnosis are ruled by fear and ritual. They are afraid that if they do not wash their hands repeatedly, count the tile squares in the floor, or something similar, something bad will happen to them or their loved ones. They gain little or no relief from obeying their compulsions, but they continue their rituals even when it tears their lives apart.

Most in health care view OCD as a lifelong affliction. They also say it is likely to be, at least in part, an inherited or genetic problem.[7] It is the kind of problem that fits a genetically determined view of life and medicine.

Dr. Jeffrey Schwartz has written about his experience with OCD patients. His work has shown that patients who change the way they think about OCD and their actions can change their outcome. While Schwartz believes that these people are born different in the way their brains process information, he does not believe they are doomed to be slaves to their compulsions.

Schwartz illustrates this on the cover of his book with the brain scans of people diagnosed with OCD. He shows their Magnetic Resonance Imaging brain scan pictures taken before they undergo therapy and afterwards. These scans show how the brain interacts with contrast material injected in order to demonstrate brain func-

---

[6]Stephen Rose, "The Rise of Neurogenetic Determinism," 380.
[7]Paul Ciechanowski, Wayne Katon, "Obsessive-compulsive Disorder: Epidemiology, clinical manifestations, and diagnosis," *UpToDate*, (5/25/2012) 1, www.uptodate.com . These articles are revised and updated every six months.

tion changes during treatment.[8] The treatment is a drug-free, four-step method that is a variation on cognitive-behavioral therapy. As a result of the therapy, the thinking, behavior, and brain scan images of patients change for the better. Schwartz's research shows that people with OCD who choose to think and act differently as they confront this problem *can* change.[9]

Old Dogs, New Tricks

The notion that the human personality is locked into a predetermined pattern of behavior comes in part from the belief that our brains have finished developing and changing by the time we reach adulthood. In the last century, there were two opposing views on this subject.

On one side was William James,[10] who believed that "organic matter, especially nervous tissue, seems endowed with a very extraordinary degree of plasticity." When James proposed that the brain had "a structure weak enough to yield to an influence," he was siding with those who believe that our behavior can change. He would not have been surprised by Hannah's spiritual and emotional recovery.

On the other side of the argument was Santiago Ramón y Cajal, who won the Nobel Prize for medicine in 1906. Unlike James, Cajal said in 1913 that "in the adult centers the nerve paths are something fixed, ended and immutable."[11] Cajal's viewpoint prevailed for nearly a century. It fit the concept that depression and other mood and behavior disorders were genetic and chemical. Though I disagree with Cajal's view, it is completely understandable that he, along with others in neurology and psychiatry, would think as they did.

---

[8] Jeffrey Schwartz, *Brain Lock* (New York: Harper-Collins/Regan Books, 1997), xxii. See back cover.

[9] Ibid., xxiii.

[10] Sharon Begley, (2008–11–12). *Train Your Mind, Change Your Brain: How a New Science Reveals Our Extraordinary Potential to Transform Ourselves* (New York: Ballantine Books, Kindle Edition), 5. "William James, the father of experimental psychology in the United States, first introduced the word *plasticity* to the science of the brain . . . in 1890." Begley has written an excellent book documenting current research in the field of brain plasticity. It is written in the context of her religious views.

[11] Ibid., 4.

When Cajal made his observations, the scientific understanding of the human brain and mind was limited to what could be observed in the patient and seen at an autopsy. When Cajal said that nerves and neurons were "fixed," he was probably looking at a patient who had suffered a stroke or spinal cord injury from which there could be little or no recovery. At autopsy, he could see the damage that resulted in the loss of function. It would have been hard to arrive at any other conclusion with the technology available at the time. But technology has progressed and the glass we look through is much clearer these days.

Plastic or Stone: You Choose!

What Cajal could not know (because he could not see it) was that our brains are more changeable or plastic than anyone could have imagined. Functional magnetic resonance imaging (fMRI) and positron emission tomography (PET) scanning allow us to see not only brain structure but brain function before, after, and sometimes during physical and mental activity.

Testing done in cancer patients to track the growth of new cancer cells has also allowed researchers to look at the growth of new neurons in the brain. In 1913, Cajal did not believe such growth could take place, but today's brains scans have shown us otherwise. Research done by Rusty Gage and Peter Eriksson conclusively showed that the human brain grows new cells.

In their study they wrote, "All of the brains had evidence of new cells. . . . And we could prove through chemical analysis that they were mature neurons. The neurons were born in the patients when they were in their fifties and seventies." They found that between 500 to 1000 new neural stem cells were born every day, when the brain was supposed to be fixed and unchanging.[12]

So, far from being set in stone, our brain tissue is designed to change. This challenges some of the assumptions about depression, worry, and other mood and behavior disorders. In addition to the simple replacement of old neurons with new, our brains also

[12]Sharon Begley, *Train Your Mind, Change Your Brain*, 64–65.

change in response to our experiences. In 1995, researchers studied the visual areas of the brain in blind people who read Braille. They found that the brain's visual cortex would light up on functional MRIs when the people were reading with their fingers! This meant that the Braille-reader's brain was using the visual cortex area to augment what the fingertips were doing in reading.[13] The way the brain functioned changed because of the way it was being used.

This is not an isolated research finding. In another study that looked at the changes in the brains of students who learned and practiced piano scales, researchers found that the area of the brain that controlled the fingers as they did the scales expanded at the expense of the areas around it. That is, the brain changed in response to the students' actions. The researchers took the study one step further and had some of the participants simply think about doing scales, literally practicing in their minds without using their hands.

They found that simply thinking through the scales had the same effect as physically doing them: it expanded the space of the brain used in the task. The researchers concluded that "mental practice alone may be sufficient to promote the plastic modulation of neural circuits."[14] The human brain has been designed with the ability to adapt to physical and mental experiences. It appears that how we think, feel, and act all can shape our brain. This challenges the notion that depression is an inescapable, genetically-caused emotional disorder. As Christians, none of this should surprise us. The change that came in Hannah's life was not an isolated event. Paul was not the exception among those who followed Christ. Instead he would become more the rule.

Christianity: New Things Are Coming!

One consistent theme in the New Testament is that Christians change. It is the very essence of the faith. By his grace, God saves us and graciously makes us his workmanship (Eph. 2:8–10). It is *really good news*! It has been good news for two millennia because

---

[13]Sharon Begley, *Train Your Mind, Change Your Brain,* 92.
[14]Ibid., 152.

most of us come to Christ looking for a way out of the mud in which we have gotten ourselves stuck.

We are people a lot like Hannah. We live with sadness born out of disappointments and losses. And, like Hannah, we do not have to spend our lives believing that we have nothing to look forward to but sadness.

It is true that we are people lost in a desert, dying of thirst. We are tired, weary, and carrying heavy burdens. We are slaves to destructive habits. We are consumed with worry about our problems, the problems of others and how they will affect us. We live in a society consumed with materialism and worry that we will not get what we deserve. The Bible describes us as dead in trespasses and sins. That is the bad news. The good news is that we are not doomed to stay that way.

Instead of biological-genetic determinism deciding our future, the consistent message of Christianity is that "if anyone is in Christ, he is a new creature; the old things passed away; behold, new things have come" (2 Cor. 5:17). Our thoughts and behavior are not unavoidably decided for us by our brains. The Bible says, "As [a man] thinks in his heart, so is he" (Prov. 23:7 KJV). Instead of being ruled by biologically dictated thoughts, we can hide God's Word in our hearts to avoid sin (Ps. 119:11). Instead of being chained to an unhappy, uncertain future, Jesus promises us, "If you continue in My word, *then* you are truly disciples of Mine; and you will know the truth, and the truth will make you free" (John 8:31–32).

This chapter started with two questions: Why do we "need" to turn sadness into depression? Why do we "need" to believe that it is a permanent state? The answer seems to be that as a nation we have turned our backs on the one source of good answers to the problems we face. Because of that, we struggle with heavy burdens. The truly good news comes from Jesus when he says, "Come to Me, all who are weary and heavy-laden, and I will give you rest. Take My yoke upon you and learn from Me, for I am gentle and humble in heart, and you will find rest for your souls. For My yoke is easy and My burden is light" (Matt. 11:28–30).

If Hannah had lived in our culture and sought relief for her grief according to our society's standard of care, she would have been worse off. The answer she needed was more than a solution to her infertility and her marital problems. She needed God to meet her and change her heart. When Hannah recognized that, she changed. The good news of the gospel is that the same opportunity exists for us.

So far, we have seen that much of what is identified as depression is likely to be normal sadness over loss. We have also seen that sadness is a normal response God designed to drive us to himself. While sadness is being reclassified as a mood disorder today, we have found that it is not necessarily a disease we are genetically fated to endure. Instead, a growing body of science indicates that we have a choice in the matter. In the next chapter we will see what the Scriptures say about that choice. We will look at another young woman who, like Hannah, chose joy after mourning.

9

Living by Grace Instead of Labels

When we first encountered Hannah, she was struggling with "no." At first, God's answer to Hannah's prayers and heart's desire to have children was no. It drove her to despair, to God, and eventually to change by grace. Hannah is not the only biblical example of someone who struggled with a problem for which the answer was no.

What happens when we don't get what we want? Can we adapt to the circumstance and still find our way out of the sorrow? Those are good questions and there is a good answer. When Paul told us to "be imitators of me, just as I also am of Christ" (1 Cor. 11:1), I doubt he had any idea just how widely it could be applied. Paul had some kind of physical problem. We do not know what it was, but we know it was troublesome enough to cause him to ask God to do something about it.

He called it a "thorn in the flesh." "Concerning this I implored the Lord three times that it might leave me" (2 Cor. 12:8). You might think that the man who wrote more of the New Testament than anyone else could get a break here, wouldn't you? He had important things to do, places to go, people who needed him, and this thorn was keeping him from it all. So he asked God three times for relief. Just as Hannah went down to the temple year after year and begged God, so Paul got down on his knees and asked for healing.

And three times God said, "No."

No?

At the age of twenty-one, "Eve" was a junior at a major midwestern university. Things were going well until she was suddenly struck down with a life-threatening illness. She survived the initial episode with a long and painful hospitalization. But the problem she faced after leaving the hospital was probably worse, as far as she was concerned.

She was told that her ailment could return at any time and that when it did, it could be fatal. The doctors could not tell her with certainty that she would be well or that she would die. They could only speak in terms of possibilities and percentages when she sought assurance that life would again go on normally.

The dreadful uncertainty was killing her. Her mood went from fear to anger to resentment and bitterness and finally to depression. Things that had been important to her before her illness no longer seemed to matter. School no longer commanded her attention. She had been an A student but now she did not bother to go to class or do the course work. She hovered between mediocrity and failure.

Eve had been raised in a home that valued the Christian faith. She had attended church regularly, read her Bible daily, and prayed often before the dark hopelessness settled in on her. Now she avoided these things and began to experiment with self-medication. Despite being at a school where drinking and drunkenness were considered normal pastimes, Eve had never participated in any of it until after her illness. For a time, she got drunk as often as she could and still survive. Life just did not worry her so much after a six-pack.

Eve struggled with sleep unless she drank herself into a stupor. Her appetite was gone and her friends had a hard time finding her. There was really nothing she enjoyed doing anymore. Young men who had seemed interesting to her no longer attracted her attention. All of this floated on the rising tide of her drinking.

After some time, like the Prodigal Son, she came to herself. As unhappy as she was, Eve knew she could not continue to live that way for long. In her own strength she stopped drinking and then came to see me. She had seen the edge of the abyss and was frightened, anxious, struggling with a depressed mood, and looking for help. By the time she sat across from me, she had fully recovered medically, but she was convinced that she had another medical disease that was making her very sad.

Eve poured out her story to me. While her illness had kept her in the hospital for less than two weeks, its aftermath had cost her an entire semester of school. After she recovered from the initial fright, she became angry and resentful of the problem she faced. She did not think it was fair that she should lose half a year out of school. She had dreams and goals. She wanted to finish school, find Mr. Right, become Mrs. Right and move on to career, home, cars, and children. Her disease stood in the way and might even prevent all those things.

Eventually, Eve began to believe that God did not care about her problems, so she decided that living according to the principles she had been raised with was a waste of time. This led to her drinking and her near failure in school. But all of this was getting her nowhere near where she wanted to be in life. The question she asked me was simple. "Is my bad mood a disease, or is there something I can do about it?" Eve needed hope and help.

Is This Sadness or Disease?

Paul and Eve had much in common. They both suffered with a physical ailment. They spent time asking God to deliver them from the trouble. Neither of them was. That is where the similarities end and the important differences begin.

Paul and Eve part ways someplace after the onset of their symptoms. Eve recovered physically but struggled with uncertainty. Eve wanted to have life in some controllable order that was out of her reach. Because of that, Eve's life spun out of control into the depths of sadness.

Paul responded to the problem differently, though it is safe to say that he suffered as much as Eve. He described it like this.

> Because of the surpassing greatness of the revelations, for this reason, to keep me from exalting myself, there was given me a thorn in the flesh, a messenger of Satan to torment me—to keep me from exalting myself! Concerning this I implored the Lord three times that it might leave me.
>
> —2 Corinthians 12:7–10

This does not sound like a common cold. Paul said it was a messenger of Satan, a thorn in his flesh, and he begged God to remove it. Eve suffered, but most of her physical suffering was over in a couple of weeks. It is likely that Paul lived with his pain for years. What made the difference? As Hannah's name told us, it was grace.

Grace Makes All the Difference

What kept Paul from tumbling into the dark sadness we call depression today? Paul had a couple of advantages over Eve. They were advantages Eve could have used, and they are available to us all. Eve did not use them simply because she did not know about them.

At some point, Paul understood why he had his thorn. Paul said he had been caught up into heaven and, while there, he heard things he could not express because God would not allow it (2 Cor. 12:1–6). Paul does not say when this happened, but some people refer to the time he was stoned at Iconium and left for dead (Acts 14:9). At any rate, Paul had seen heaven and heard heavenly things.

"Because of the surpassing greatness of the revelations," Paul was *given* his thorn so that he would not "exalt himself." Pride evidently was a potential problem for Paul and God gave him the thorn to help him avoid it. Perhaps you are thinking, "That's just great. Paul has a potential character issue and so he gets a thorn." But it doesn't end there. Paul also gets grace.

Three times Paul asks for relief from his painful struggle. Three times God answers him, "My grace is sufficient for you, for power is perfected in weakness" (2 Cor. 12:9). This is not the "Get out of jail free" card we often hope for when faced with serious difficulty. This is the "I will bring you through this" card we desperately need when we suffer pain or watch the bottom fall out of life. It made all the difference in how Paul responded to his thorn. Instead of sadness, Paul chose gladness.

> Most gladly, therefore, I will rather boast about my weaknesses, that the power of Christ may dwell in me. Therefore I am well content with weaknesses, with insults, with distresses, with persecutions, with difficulties, for Christ's sake; for when I am weak, then I am strong.
> —2 Corinthians 12: 9–10

Gladly, Paul says! It would have been great if God had chosen to heal Paul on the spot. I'll bet he would have boasted about that just as enthusiastically. But Paul knew that while his illness or trouble made him physically weak, it made room *in* him for Christ's power, and he was really glad about that. I am *content*, Paul said, with weakness, insults, distress, persecution and difficulty for the sake of Jesus because when he was physically weak, Christ's power made him strong.

I don't think for a minute that Paul enjoyed suffering any more than the rest of us. His suffering was real, just like it was for Hannah, Martha, Mary, Lazarus, and the woman with the hemorrhage. But he gladly endured the pain because he loved Jesus. Paul loved Jesus because Jesus had first loved him.

As Paul said, "But God demonstrates His own love toward us, in that while we were yet sinners, Christ died for us" (Rom. 5:8). In light of that, Paul chose to gladly suffer. What we learn from Paul's suffering is that when God intends us to do anything, his grace will be present to enable us to do his will. Paul was *given* his thorn by God and he was also given grace. Eve did not understand any of this, so that was the point of the counseling we did together—to help her see God's purposes and grace in her life.

Someone might object to using Paul as a role model by saying something like, "Hey, Paul was an apostle and he wrote part of the Bible. I would expect him to do well with suffering!" The question is whether Hannah's and Paul's experiences translate into something that can help someone like Eve. The answer is yes. Paul's story includes important things Eve needed to understand in order to deal with the suffering generated by our trials.

Eve's Thorny Grace: Choosing Not to Live by Labels

When I met Eve, she was in perfect health but absolutely convinced that she was going to die. To my knowledge, she has been in good health since her initial illness. It was not the reality of her health that was causing her trouble. Her depressed mood did not grow out of a chemical imbalance or physical disease. It was caused by the way she looked at her problem and responded to it.

Certainly, most mental health professionals would have diagnosed Eve as depressed. But the first time I talked with her, I chose not to label her. Instead, we started on a journey that would let Eve adapt to the circumstances that brought her into sadness. After she finished her story, her first question to me was, "Do I have depression?" I had a choice that day. I could have given Eve a medical label that offered little hope. Instead, I decided her counseling would not be determined by a label. I responded by saying that we would discuss that later. If Eve was going to escape her sadness, there were more pressing things to discuss.

The first thing she needed to know was that God knew and cared about her illness, worry, and suffering just like he did Paul's. God cared just as much about Eve as he did about Hannah or Martha. So Eve and I read the account Paul gave of his suffering to the Corinthians, where he said that it is God who comforts us in all our affliction so that we will be able to comfort others (2 Cor. 1:3–4).

Eve needed to see the deliberate pattern of care that Jesus gave his friends Martha, Mary, and Lazarus. As we studied the account in John, she saw that just as Jesus knew about Lazarus, Jesus knew about her problems. She learned that Jesus had a plan and that he cared and wept for her. On that first visit, it was important for her to understand that Jesus listened without judgment to the heartfelt cry of his friends. Eve learned that Jesus cared about Eve just as he did Martha, Mary, and Lazarus. Jesus knew about every pain, every stitch, every needle and every minute of every day she considered lost.

The next place Eve needed to go was to 1 Corinthians 10. In that chapter she faced the question that is generally beneath the anger that drives much sadness. Eve wanted to know "Why?" Why me? Why this? Why now? Why do I have to deal with the great cosmic "No" that I can't be healthy and have all the things I want when I want them?

The story in 1 Corinthians 10 describes the grave misstep the children of Israel made while wandering in the desert after leaving Egypt. They had watched God part the Red Sea, walked through it on dry ground, drank water from the rock God commanded Moses to strike, and still managed to fall into idol worship while Moses was on Sinai getting the Ten Commandments. Their problem is not difficult to see. They wanted a god they could push around on a cart, one they could see and touch. They would rather worship a thing than the God who brought them out of the slavery of Egypt.

Eve had a variant strain of the idolatry virus. She did not want to worship a golden calf, she just wanted her health—and she wanted a god who would give it to her. Eve had to choose between that idol and the true God if she ever wanted to have joy instead of sadness. She had been demanding a god who would meet her demand for immediate healing and deliverance. The real God offered a different solution to her problem in verse 13.

No temptation has overtaken you but such as is common to man; and God is faithful, who will not allow you to be tempted beyond what you are able, but with the temptation will provide the way of escape also, so that you will be able to endure it.

—1 Corinthians 10:13

"This is a test, this is only a test!" Just as the children of Israel faced a test at the foot of Sinai, Eve faced the same test about idolatry. What are you going to worship? Eve saw that her illness was not special. By that I do not mean that it wasn't painful or that her suffering was not real. But she was not alone in it. Thousands of people suffer like her every day. Illness is common to us all. At the same time, Eve saw that God was being faithful to her just as Jesus was to Lazarus. He would make a way through it so that she could bear up under it. By God's amazing grace, he intended to empower Eve to bear up under the load.

But the choice would be hers and its ramifications are reflected in Paul's words in verse 31: "Whether, then, you eat or drink or whatever you do, do all to the glory of God" (1 Cor. 10:31). The choice for Eve and any of us who suffer loss is whether or not we will glorify God in the process. Worship him or worship health?

When we finished 1 Corinthians 10, we had one more concept to consider: motive. When people talk to me about their struggles, eventually we must talk about their goal in doing so. It is not much of a surprise if they say they want to feel better. I don't blame them at all for thinking that way. Whenever I have been in real, unremitting pain, I find myself looking for relief like everyone else.

But Eve had struggled long without much progress. She had devoted months to finding relief. She realized that it had become her main goal in life, her motive for living. That day I told Eve that I believed she could recover fully from her sadness/depression, but she would have to be willing to change her goal. Her goal had been relief from her burden. But from that moment forward, her motive would be summed up in one sentence:

I want to glorify God with my life more than I want to breathe.

The first person I shared that sentence with struggled with a depressed mood and was starving herself to death. Eve and that woman had one thing in common. They wanted something in life and they weren't going to be happy until they had it. I derived that sentence from something Paul said in his second letter to the Corinthians: "Therefore we also have as our ambition, whether at home or absent, to be pleasing to Him" (2 Cor. 5:9). I told Eve what I have repeated to hundreds of fellow strugglers in the last ten years: "You must be willing to say, 'I want to glorify God with my life more than I want to breathe.' That's it. That's all you have to do."

Of course, for Eve that meant she had to want to glorify God with her life more than she wanted to be healthy. She had to want to glorify God more than she wanted back the half-year she had lost. She had to want to glorify God more than she wanted to be safe from a relapse. The list could go on, but in the end Eve would have to give up worshiping what she wanted and instead worship God.

Love God More!

It might seem a little abrupt to say this to someone so overcome with sadness, but Eve wasn't in the hospital anymore and this had been going on for months. For Eve, the situation was a lot like when Jesus was in the graveyard. The time for weeping was over and it was time to roll the stone off the grave. And so we did. The next thing Eve needed to know was that it is God who decides what it means to glorify him. So I asked her to read what Jesus said when someone asked him what the great commandment was.

> "YOU SHALL LOVE THE LORD YOUR GOD WITH ALL YOUR HEART, AND WITH ALL YOUR SOUL, AND WITH ALL YOUR MIND. This is the great and foremost commandment. The second is like it, YOU SHALL LOVE YOUR NEIGHBOR AS YOURSELF."
>
> —Matthew 22:37–39

There it is, as plain as day from the lips of God. If Eve wanted to glorify God with her life, she must love God with all her heart, soul, and mind. That meant she had to love God more than health, safety, school, husband, children, houses, cars and anything else she could possibly think of. She had to love God more!

Love Me? Obey Me!

Just as it is God who decides what it means to glorify him, it is God who decides what it means for us to love him. Again, from the lips of God the Son, Eve heard what God thinks it looks like when someone loved him.

He who has My commandments and keeps them is the one who loves Me; and he who loves Me will be loved by My Father, and I will love him and will disclose Myself to him.

—John 14:21

This is really straightforward and not surprising. Jesus went on to say that if we love him we will keep his word, and that if we do not keep his word we do not love him (John 14:23–25). Again Jesus says plainly, "If you love Me, you will keep My commandments" (John 14:15).

Eve had started doing many things when she became disappointed with the turn her life had taken. In that first visit, I did not give her the list, but it included her anger, fear, worry, drunkenness, laziness, bitterness, and her avoidance of church, her Bible, and prayer. Instead, I asked her a simple question. If the Bible says something about what you are doing, will you agree to obey what it says? Eve was a Christian and she was desperate, so she agreed that she would.

What came next was very important. I told Eve that she would never be alone in doing whatever the Bible said she must do. The grace of God that saved her from her sin would be the same grace that would enable her to abandon the sins she had been practicing since her illness struck.

Again, Jesus told us (and Eve) that the key to growth and change would be in our connection to him.

"Abide in Me, and I in you. As the branch cannot bear fruit of itself unless it abides in the vine, so neither can you unless you abide in Me. I am the vine, you are the branches; he who abides in Me and I in him, he bears much fruit, for apart from Me you can do nothing."

—John 15:4–5

Eve was not going to be forced into a relationship with Christ in which she would spend her life working hard to please him but never know if it was good enough. Instead, Eve was part of the body of Christ, the church, and as she drew near to Jesus, she would abide in him and he would abide in her. Then her life would bear much fruit.

As Eve read Scripture and saw the changes God commanded, she could come to God in prayer and ask for grace.

> For we do not have a high priest who cannot sympathize with our weaknesses, but One who has been tempted in all things as we are, yet without sin. Therefore let us draw near with confidence to the throne of grace, so that we may receive mercy and find grace to help in time of need.
>
> —Hebrew 4:15–16

Eve would not have to face her anger, fear, worry, greed, laziness, or any other sin alone. She would have grace. She would find, as Paul said, that it would be "God who is at work in [her], both to will and to work for His good pleasure" (Phil. 2:13). She could depend on the fact that, as a Christian, she could "do all things through Him who strengthens me" (Phil. 4:13). Change might not be easy, but it would be possible, powered by God's grace.

No More Navel-Gazing!

Now Eve had a different reason or motive for doing things in life. Instead of mourning the loss she had suffered, her life could now head in a different direction. The losses could not change, since they were in the past. But what she did with her time now *could* change.

There was one last thing to cover in our meeting. Over time, Eve had become extremely focused on her own problems and needs. She spent most of her waking hours thinking about her desire to be healthy. The change had come so gradually that she barely noticed it, but Eve had become amazingly self-centered. If she was going to escape the sadness that had come with her losses, she was going to have to switch her focus from herself to other people. In the next chapter we will see how Eve was able to do just that.

10

Changing Behavior and Changing Moods

The connection between the way Eve thought about her problems and the way she felt was clear. She believed her illness was a disaster without a purpose and her mood reflected her anger, fear, worry, and depression. But there was more to her problem than the way she was thinking. Eve's behavior had a significant impact on her mood as well. As we worked on the heart issues that drove her behavior, there were things Eve needed to change.

Eve was in the place where many who struggle with a sad mood find themselves. She was much like Mary and Martha in the graveyard of life. Eve needed to know that Jesus cared about her just as he did Martha and Mary, and that he had a plan for her life. But most of all she needed a sense of direction and a way to tackle her problems.

After Mary and Jesus wept, it was time to roll away the stone. It was time to leave the graveyard. For Eve, this would mean changing the thinking and behavior that reinforced her bad mood. The things I would tell her would be practical and very specific.

Behaving and Feeling

The connection between how we feel and how we act has been evident since creation. The Bible has many illustrations of this relationship. The fear that Adam and Eve suffered as they hid from God in the garden was directly connected to their decision to eat the forbidden fruit. That behavior caused an estrangement from God that was accompanied by guilt, fear, and sadness over loss.

Throughout King Saul's reign, his rebellious choices haunted him like Scrooge's Christmas ghosts. Saul simply could not wait for Samuel to make a sacrifice and it cost him his job (1 Sam. 13:1–14). Saul would not carry out the mission God gave him to destroy the Amalekites and it eventually cost him his life (1 Sam. 15:19–23). Between that time and his death at the hands of the Philistines, Saul spent most of his time unhappy, sleepless, and fearful. His only amusement seemed to be trying to kill David. For Saul, choosing to do wrong made him emotionally miserable.

God's chosen people Israel illustrate the problem too. When they served God and obeyed his commandments, they prospered. When they disobeyed God and worshiped idols, they suffered. Isaiah relayed God's message to them.

> "If only you had paid attention to My commandments! Then your well-being would have been like a river, And your righteousness like the waves of the sea."
>
> —Isaiah 48:18

If only! If only they had chosen to obey and do what they knew to be right. Instead they chose to do wrong and that sense of well-being went right out the window. In place of well-being, the children of Israel got another message from God through Isaiah.

> "There is no peace for the wicked," says the LORD.
>
> —Isaiah 48:22

By the time Eve and I talked, she fit this model. Eve had no peace and in its place she had worry, fear, anger, and a very dark mood. By the time I saw her, a lot of her trouble was directly connected to the things she knew she should not be doing. The rest came from the important things she was neglecting. To help her out of her darkness, Eve needed to change the way she was acting as well as the way she thought.

Washing Dirty Feet

Eve and I looked to the account of the Last Supper in John's gospel to give her the direction she was going to need. The events occur just hours before Jesus was betrayed by Judas to those who wanted him killed. It would be the last meal Jesus would eat and from it would come the Christian practice of Communion. Remarkably, John does not refer to the bread and the cup that Jesus would pass around, saying, "This do in remembrance of me." What John did record was Jesus washing dirty feet (John 13).

At the time, any good dinner party required a servant to stand near the front door and wash the feet of the incoming guests. The reason was very practical. Most people walked wherever they went and there was no indoor plumbing or garbage collection. Human waste and garbage were thrown into the street. A dinner guest had to walk through that muck to get there and, while he might be clean from the ankles up, his or her feet probably stunk. So a host would put a servant at the door to wash their feet.

Jesus had sent a couple of disciples ahead to make the necessary preparations for the meal. All was ready. There was a bowl with water and a towel, but there was no servant at the door. I wonder what it was like that evening to be reclining at the table, waiting for someone else to get up and wash the feet. I suspect it was awkward as the group tried to determine the least worthy person to use the bowl and towel. So no one moved.

Then Jesus stood, took off his cloak, wrapped the towel around himself and took the bowl. Then he started washing stinky, dirty feet. The Lord of Glory was serving men who would not serve each other. He came to Peter, who wanted to argue with Jesus about his intention to wash his feet, but Jesus in essence tells Peter to put up or shut up! Either I wash your feet or you are none of mine. Peter relented.

Jesus even washed Judas' feet, an amazing act full of significance for us. Jesus washed the feet of his enemy and still does. Then it was done. He stands up, takes the towel from around his waist, puts his coat back on and speaks.

> "Do you know what I have done to you? You call Me Teacher and Lord; and you are right, for so I am. If I then, the Lord and the Teacher, washed your feet, you also ought to wash one another's feet. For I gave you an example that you also should do as I did to you. Truly, truly, I say to you, a slave is not greater than his master, nor is one who is sent greater than the one who sent him. If you know these things, you are blessed[1] if you do them."
>
> —John 13:12–17

The message for Eve and for anyone in her situation is so full of hope! Do you want to exchange your sadness for joy? Then do what Jesus did. Because of the new life he purchased for us on the cross, we have the Holy Spirit to enable us to follow Jesus in this way. Ask Jesus to change your heart. Humble yourself and serve others. Stop worshiping your own comfort and focus on the comfort of others. That is what Jesus did when he refused to think of his own needs, but instead thought about ours.

The only way to have happiness or joy in this life is found in serving Jesus and others instead of serving self. So Jesus said, "Now that you know these things, happy are you if you do them." For the Christian, the most direct way to exchange sorrow for this blessed, joyful happiness is to do what you know the Scriptures say we should.

Eve *knew* better. Yes, that was the best way to say it. She was doing things she *knew* would cause her trouble. That was bad news and good news at the same time. It was bad that she had chosen

---

[1] The Greek word in the text is *makarios* and is translated as "happy" in other versions of the New Testament.

to do these things and she had the emotional bruises to show for it. It was good news because she could change what she was *doing.*

Changing Behavior, Changing Feelings

There were lots of practical things Eve needed to do to escape her dark mood. Until Eve was stricken with her illness, she had been a well-organized, hard-working young woman. By the time I saw her, she wasn't doing her schoolwork or taking care of her space in her apartment. Most people would say she had gone from a clean freak to messy in record time. She was not paying attention to her personal hygiene and appearance. Diet and exercise were in a similar state of neglect.

Her spiritual state was just as sorry. She was not attending church, reading her Bible, praying, or having fellowship with other believers. She was alone in her spiritual wasteland. She neglected friends and ignored the care and interest of family.

Almost all of it ended on our second visit. It had to end. It was not a matter of applying legalistic rules with a guarantee of a better mood in exchange for compliance. Eve was living in slothful sin and she needed to repent and change whether she felt better or not. The words of Jesus from John 13:17 were forcefully applied: "Now that you know these things, happy are you if you do them."

If Eve had chosen the opposite response, Jesus' words could have been applied this way: You know these things but you are unhappily not doing them! As the writer of Proverbs said, "He that covers his sin shall not prosper, but whoever confesses and forsakes it will have mercy" (Prov. 28:13, author's paraphrase). Eve needed to change her habits because she would never feel good until she did. Nobody would!

So that day, because Eve agreed that she wanted to glorify God with her life more than she wanted to breathe, I gave her a number of assignments. She would have to do them whether she felt like it or not. Doing them would not guarantee her recovery from her depressed mood. But her mood and her health were no longer her primary goal in life. Glorifying God was her primary goal and she could not live as she had been and glorify God. Doing her assignments might not be easy at first, but Eve had the assurance that God would provide her gracious help when she needed it.

Return to the Normals

There is a lot to be said for a "normal" routine in life. That routine is made up of lots of things I like to call "the normals." Exercise is one of them. A recent published study showed that women who exercised more and watched less television were 20 percent less likely to get depressed than their couch potato counterparts. The study indicated that "physical activity is important to maintaining brain health."[2] The sad thing about the study was the amount of money that was spent to find out something that common sense might have predicted.

So Eve got back on the road again. She started walking and worked her way up from fifteen minutes a day to forty-five minutes. Her television and recreational computer use were limited to thirty minutes a day. Instead of hours of mindless channel surfing fueled by thousands of calories of junk food and soda, Eve would have more time for personal hygiene, laundry, and cleaning. (Her roommate was truly grateful!) She also had to eat a normal three square meals a day.

Other neglected normals were resumed. She returned to all of her classes and did all of her work. When she came for her appointment with me every week, I would be asking about her compliance and she expected it.

Eve also returned to her church and not just for sixty minutes on Sunday morning. She became part of a small group that met on Sunday after church, made up of other college-age young people. Eve had to take notes on the sermon and on the lesson discussed in her small group and bring them to her weekly session with me. Eve needed active listening, not passive compliance with a rule.

Fellowship with other believers was vital to Eve's growth. But I challenged her not to view the time she spent with the small group as valuable only if *she* got something out of it. Eve needed to see

---

[2]Genevra Pittman, "Too little exercise, too much TV tied to depression," *Reuter's Health* (Nov. 13, 2001) www.reuters.com (11/16/2011).

it as an opportunity to minister to others. Others in that group needed fellowship and Eve could serve them in that way. Instead of seeking her own good, she would be seeking the good of others (see 1 Cor. 10:24). I told Eve that she could not hide from her friends. If friends asked her to go somewhere or do something, she had to go unless she had a compelling reason to decline.

An obvious normal that Eve had neglected was her study of the Scriptures. I asked her to read one chapter a day in the gospel of John to start. I told her that eventually it would be good for her to read three chapters a day and four on Sunday, which would allow her to read the Bible once a year. Time spent in daily prayer was essential to her growth in grace. I suggested that, in addition to praise, confession, and bringing her own requests before the Lord, she should develop a list of people she prayed for regularly. In addition, I assigned at least one verse a week for Eve to memorize. We would pick verses that would help her escape her dark mood.

It was no surprise to me that Eve's mood improved when she resumed normal living. The habits she had gotten into because she was unhappy would have depressed most of us, even if we did not have any problems. There was one last aspect of her behavior that needed to change and it had a profound effect on her mood.

Washing Dirty Feet Part II

From the onset of her illness until the time I met her, Eve's life was consumed by her own problems. There was no room for concern about anyone else. But as I talked with her about the fact that Christians are supposed to serve others just as Jesus washed the feet of the disciples, I stressed that doing something about that knowledge would be a big help to her. So, for the first time since her illness, Eve was going to do a Christian service assignment.

Thirty-five years ago, I read an article by a well-known psychologist and physician[3] that shaped my views on this subject. In it, an

---

[3]Dr. George Crane wrote a syndicated column called "The Worry Clinic" that appeared in my local newspaper. Born in 1901, Crane's career included writing speeches for President Calvin Coolidge. He wrote a psychology textbook, *Psychology Applied*, that was published from 1932

elderly physician told the newspaper columnist that when he had patients who were depressed, he told them to walk two miles a day, to read one chapter of the gospel of Luke each day and to help someone else for two hours a week. Here the doctor became very specific.

The person to be helped needed to be worse off than the depressed patient. This person could not be a relative (since there is almost always secondary gain in doing something for your mother-in-law) and the depressed person could take nothing from the person he or she helped. The assistance had to be for a person, not a task like washing windows at the church. And this assignment was to continue indefinitely.

Of all the things the elderly physician told the young psychologist-columnist, this last point may have been the most helpful. The primary benefit of this service to others was to get the patient focused on the needs of others. For example, it would be hard for Eve to be bitter about her illness while helping a child with leukemia at a local hospital.

Eve's Christian service assignment turned out to be an elderly lady living alone. She needed help with lots of things, but most of all she needed to know that someone in the world cared about her. Every week Eve went and did chores around the house and then sat and talked to the woman, whose physical limitations kept her mostly at home. The more she went, the more Eve appreciated her current health and the less she thought about her prior illness.

Know, Do, Happy!

Eve still had other problems to face, but at least now she understood the relationship between her heart attitude, the things she did, and the way she felt. She knew that she must be a "doer of the word and not a hearer only" (James 1:22). Just as her unbiblical actions had made her emotional situation worse, her biblical actions now helped.

It would not have been possible to help Eve out of her trouble by artificially dividing her into her thinking, acting, and emotional

to 1967. He was best known for writing on marital subjects. The source for this information was www.wikipedia.org. Crane died July 17, 1995.

parts. Those three aspects of her personhood were working together in her life—and not working well until she decided to change all of them. As noted earlier, Eve had a problem with anger. To deal with the corrosive emotions that came with anger, she needed to settle the argument she was having with God. Eve would need the same kind of confrontation that Martha and Mary had with Jesus on the way to the graveyard.

11

Settling an Argument

Eve was making progress with her thoughts, emotions, and behavior, but she did have an argument she needed to settle. The reason Eve had neglected the normal duties of life was that she was angry with God. Where was he when she was suffering? While she struggled with that question, anger grew into bitterness and bitterness then was used to justify the way she chose to live. At some point Eve went from suffering to using that suffering to justify living in a way that disobeyed, even rebelled, against God.

If Eve was going to emerge from the struggle she had with her moods, she needed to look at her sadness and suffering in a different way. She needed different definitions of sadness and suffering and we found them in Paul's second letter to the Corinthians.

When Paul wrote his first letter to the Christians at Corinth, the church was in real trouble because of the sin they were tolerating. Paul's letter was a stinging rebuke and a call for them to repent and change. And the church did. They excluded a member who was living in adultery and he repented. However, the church refused to restore the man to their fellowship afterwards. So Paul wrote a second letter.

In that letter, Paul talks about the sorrow and sadness he had caused the Corinthians with his earlier rebuke. He more or less says that he wasn't unhappy about it at all. The church had repented, and for that Paul was glad, no matter how much grief they had suffered. So Paul wrote as follows:

> I now rejoice, not that you were made sorrowful, but that you were made sorrowful to the point of repentance; for you were made sorrowful according to the will of God, so that you might not suffer loss in anything through us. For the sorrow that is according to the will of God produces a repentance without regret, leading to salvation, but the sorrow of the world produces death.
>
> —2 Corinthians 7:9–10

When we lose things, it generally brings sorrow that can go in one of two directions. We can manage our sadness the same way the world does. That is, we can manage it like Eve, whose sadness led to anger, bitterness, and sin. Literally, her loss-induced sadness was producing deadly things in her life. She was sorrowing the way the world does.

But when Christians face loss, we have another option: to let that sorrow lead us to change and repentance. And we can choose to deal with the loss the way James advised: "Consider it all joy, my brethren, when you encounter various trials, knowing that the testing of your faith produces endurance" (James 1:2–3). Eve did not have to descend into the dark mood she suffered. She could have avoided it if she had considered her situation differently.

Sorrowing Christians Have Options

Consider is an interesting word. It's what we do as we decide what we are going to do about suffering and circumstances. We all face trials. At times they come to us because of choices we have made, and we must *consider* what God is saying to us through those trials. At times they come to us because other people sin and we happen to be in the way. Any family that has lost a loved one to a drunk driver can testify to the uninvited pain and grief. They did nothing wrong, but they suffer for another's sin. James encourages them to *consider* how they will respond to this loss in light of God's Word.

James also wants us to *consider* the trials and suffering that are not due to our sin or that of anyone else. This year in my state, good people lost homes, businesses, and loved ones to a pack of tornadoes. No individual did anything to cause them but people suffered anyway. Eve's suffering fit this category. And she might have fared far better had she taken the time to consider, as James advised.

James tells us to *consider* it all joy when we encounter trials. The Greek word γέομαι means "to think or regard." James would have us lead our minds to regard our trial as something joyful, and he has good reason to do so. The trying of our faith produces endurance and enduring the process leads to maturity.[1] This is the essence of what Jesus did as he headed to the cross. The writer of Hebrews tells us that our Savior, "for the joy set before Him, endured the cross" (Heb. 12:2).

Jesus did exactly what he calls us to do when we face a struggle. He did it on a scale so spectacular that it takes the breath out of any argument that we should do anything different. We are called to look at Jesus, who suffered and died for sins he did not commit so that we could have eternal life. Our Savior calls us to endure as he did so that we can grow.

Eve Failed to Consider

At some point when the sharp, stabbing, aching nature of Eve's pain eased, she needed to move her thinking from seeing herself as a victim to considering her trial joy. She needed to do it because of what God could be doing in her life. That was the joy Jesus had when he saw the cross and looked beyond it to see that creation would be restored and we would be saved. Instead of being focused on what she had lost, Eve needed to focus on what there was to

---

[1] Jay E. Adams, *A Thirst for Wholeness* (Woodruff, S. C.: Timeless Texts, 2006), 18. See footnote in which Adams relates that the primary meaning of the verb ἡγέομαι is to lead, with the idea that we are to lead our thoughts to the place where we consider the trial as joy because of the outcome. "The nuance of leading one's thoughts was always present."

gain in becoming more like Christ. The sooner she changed her focus, the less she would suffer.

Had she done that earlier, her sorrow and struggle could have been much shorter. Instead Eve chose angry, sinful rebellion against her circumstances and against God. Instead of solving her problem by considering, she would need to reconsider—that is, repent.

Repentance is a word we often fail to understand, even in Christian circles. We usually think of it when there is a sin we are committing that we need to confess and abandon. The word "repentance" that Paul used (μετανοέω in Greek) very simply means "to change one's mind." That is how the word was used outside Christian circles. Plato used it in 500 B. C. in *Euthydemus*. He said, "I reconsidered" what he had said earlier and changed his mind[2] to say something different.[3] But for Paul, I think it meant something more.

When most people hear the word "repent" today, I don't think they think in Plato's terms. It's not likely that they think in terms of looking at the menu of life, changing their minds and picking something else. Most of us see repentance as an action that ends an episode of bad behavior. Many Christians rightly associate it with their conversion, when they confessed their sin in repentance and trusted Christ in faith for salvation. But if they see repentance as something needed only when they first became Christians, they have missed something important about the rest of their walk with Christ. Just as we can wrongly think of "grace" and "the gospel" as things we needed at the beginning of our Christian life but not as much later on, so we can wrongly see repentance as something we needed in the past and not now.

---

[2] The words "heart," "mind," "soul," and "spirit" are often used interchangeably in the Bible. In Matthew 22:37 Jesus tells us to "love the Lord your God with all your heart, and with all your soul, and with all your mind." Jesus uses all three words to perform the same function. In the words of John A. Broadus, "All these amount to the same thing, piling up different terms to show that all our faculties and affections must be occupied with love to Jehovah." See his *Commentary on the Gospel of Matthew* (Valley Forge, Pa.: Judson Press, 1886), 458.

[3] Henry Liddell, Robert Scott, *Greek English Lexicon* (New York: Oxford Press, 1843, revised multiple times to 1977), 1115. Dr. Grant Hodges pointed me to this information in Liddell and Scott. The quote from Plato is found in section 279 of *Euthydemus*. "To perceive afterward" was given as the primary meaning; "to change one's mind" was the second, and the third was "to repent."

Daily Dose of Grace and Repentance

Much has been written recently about our need to remind ourselves of the gospel—and rightly so. Elyse Fitzpatrick, in her excellent book, *Because He Loves Me,* reminds us that many of our difficulties in Christian living come because we have considered the gospel to be something that was important primarily at the time of our conversion.[4] The reality is that we need grace and the gospel every waking moment of our Christian life if we want to live in a way that honors our heavenly Father. We need it if we hope to survive! And the marvelous truth is that God has *given* us grace through his Son. He wants us to rely on it daily.

In the same way that we need to understand and depend on God's grace, we also need repentance. Loss and sorrow have a great purpose in our lives and if we do not want to spend our lives parked in a depressed mood, we need to understand how vital repentance is to our relationship to our Lord and to our way out of sadness. When I first met Eve, she needed to repent of many things. In fact, repentance was the key to leaving her bad mood behind.

Learning Repentance from the Master Teacher

Jesus used the word "repentance" or "repent" as often as anyone in Scripture. He illustrated what he meant by it in Luke 15. The setting was a dinner at the house of a religious leader. During that dinner Jesus told a parable in which an important man had invited people to a feast. When they all made excuses, the man sent out his servants to bring in people off the street to take their places. Then Jesus says, "For I tell you, none of those men who were invited shall taste of my dinner" (Luke 14:24).

The Pharisees were at the dinner to see if they could accuse Jesus of healing people on the Sabbath or some other infraction of religious law. It irked them that the common people, the tax collectors, and other assorted sinners, were listening to Jesus. They knew Jesus was speaking about them when he said they would not get into the feast. Their response was, "This man receives sinners

---

[4]Elyse Fitzpatrick, *Because He Loves Me* (Wheaton, IL.: Crossway, 2008), 25.

and eats with them!" (15:12). I suppose they thought that proved them to be right.

Jesus' response teaches us much about what repentance is. Jesus' response teaches us much about what repentance is. Jesus tells three stories, the first story he tells is the shepherd and the lost sheep (15:3-7). Ninety-nine sheep were safely accounted for. For most of us, that might have been good enough, but not for God. There was one lost sheep—probably someone like me or you. The shepherd keeps looking until he finds it. He puts it over his shoulder and carries it home. I suppose the first lesson is that God is looking for lost people and he persists until he brings them home.

The second story is about the lost coin (15:8–10), and tells of the owner seeking an object of value. And last comes the story of the Prodigal Son (15:11–32). All three stories were meant as a rebuke to the Pharisees who accused Jesus of "receiving sinners!" In the first two stories, when the owner finds what was lost, he comes home, announces the find, and tells his friends, "Rejoice with me!" Then Jesus says, "I tell you that in the same way, there will be *more* joy in heaven over one sinner who repents, than over ninety-nine righteous persons who need no repentance" (Luke 15:7). Again he strikes the Pharisees at the heart of their problem. They were rebellious sinners who didn't think they needed to repent. But the sinners Jesus received were a cause for rejoicing in heaven *because* they had repented.

Repenting Prodigals

Jesus was not done. His last story was about a young man who would define repentance in terms that even the Pharisees could not miss. The man was the younger of two sons who went to his father one day and demanded his inheritance. Inexplicably, the father gave it to him and off the son went to live in rebellion and sin of every kind. Things seemed to go well until his money ran out. Soon he found himself feeding pigs and eating the garbage he was supposed to feed them.

Then one day as he was starving, it came to him. "He came to his senses, and said, How many of my father's hired men have more than enough bread, but I am dying here with hunger! I will get up and go to my father, and will say to him, 'Father, I have sinned against heaven, and in your sight; I am no longer worthy to be called your son; make me as one of your hired men'" (Luke 15:17–19). Off the boy goes to home, father, and hope, to finish the repentance that began in the pig pen.

When he arrives, his father sees him coming and springs into action.

> But while he was still a long way off, his father saw him and felt compassion for him, and ran and embraced him and kissed him. And the son said to him, "Father, I have sinned against heaven and in your sight; I am no longer worthy to be called your son." But the father said to his slaves, "Quickly bring out the best robe and put it on him, and put a ring on his hand and sandals on his feet; and bring the fattened calf, kill it, and let us eat and celebrate; for this son of mine was dead and has come to life again; he was lost and has been found." And they began to celebrate.
> —Luke 15:20–24

Here the rejoicing was not for the return of a valuable sheep or coin that had somehow gotten lost. Here Jesus is showing the Pharisees that the rejoicing is for sinful, rebellious, filthy, pig-feeding sinners. These are the ones Jesus is looking for, and when he finds them and they return home, there is celebration in heaven. The Pharisees were in the story too. They were represented by the older brother who never came to the party because of his own self-righteousness. He stayed outside, bitter, proud, angry, and unrepentant, while the *repentant* younger brother was inside eating!

When we fail to *consider* and respond to our trial or temptation in a godly way, we will likely respond with thoughts, attitudes, and behaviors that we will need to repent of. This was Eve's position. Her faithless response to trial had led her astray in her own version of the pig pen. Repentance is a process God works in us. It brings us to our senses so that we see the dreadful truth about our situation. Then we must agree with God about our predicament, leave the sin we are in, and confess it to him with all our heart, mind, and soul. God then forgives us and restores us to fellowship, bringing an end to our spiritual suffering and starvation.

Paul described the process in his second letter to Timothy. Paul told Timothy that when we talk to people like Eve, we should speak "with gentleness correcting those who are in opposition, if perhaps God may grant them repentance leading to the knowledge of the truth, and they may come to their senses *and escape* from the snare of the devil, having been held captive by him to do his will" (2 Tim. 2:24–26). Yes, it is God who grants us repentance and it is a great gift! And one that God wants all of us to have because he is "not willing that any should perish, but that all should come to repentance" (2 Peter 3:9 KJV).

That is why the story was important for Eve (and all of us). Like many of us, Eve had become the prodigal son. She had been confronted with a choice in life when she became ill. And, like the prodigal, she was not content in her circumstances. Eve's sorrow became fear, worry, anger, and then outright rebellion. Like the prodigal, she sinned herself into emotional slavery. As she yielded herself to serve the sins that grew from her anger, she became their slave.

And Eve, like the prodigal, came to her senses. Eve needed to repent. She needed to reconsider, change her mind, and agree with God about her response to her illness and the sinful way she lived afterwards. She needed to repent of her anger against God. And so she did!

Eve's Repentance

Eve's repentance was a lot like a dam breaking. She had a large reservoir of things to confess and it started out like a small leak. Eventually it became a roaring river. Her confession started with her failure to love God more than life itself. Eve confessed that she had placed a greater value on her health than she did on God. She loved her health and the future it promised more than she loved God. She loved things like finishing school, getting a job, and owning a house; and she loved the idea of marriage and children—things that being healthy would have given her. She confessed to God that she had loved those things more than she loved him. Now she would daily endeavor to love God with all her heart, soul, mind, and strength.

Eve confessed that she was not grateful for the fact that she was alive or for the things God had allowed her to have. She confessed her envy of others who were healthy and who had the things she wanted. She confessed the specific sins she had committed, including drunkenness and the neglect of all things Christian. She confessed her neglect of Bible study, prayer, and the fellowship of her church. She confessed that she had not lived her life to glorify and honor God.

Eve confessed her worry and her fears. Finally, she confessed her sinful anger with God over her trouble. Of all her sins, this one was at the heart of her depressed mood. Eve was angry because she believed God was telling her "no." She was accusing God of allowing or causing her trouble.

If you want to take the measure of someone's character, the most direct route I can think of is to tell him no. Tell someone no and deny him something he thinks is vital to his existence. You will be amazed at how quickly most people change their attitude and mood.

Eve was angry because she could not be certain of her health. She simmered in anger because she had to miss school. She seethed because it interrupted her plan for life. She blamed God because he could have prevented it all. Eve's anger was a sin. Eve's response to her illness made her life worse. She expected her life to be miserable and she made it even more so.

Eve badly needed to *reconsider* the question Martha and Mary had to deal with and then make a choice. This choice held the key to her escape from a sad mood. The question was Martha's: "Where were you when I needed you?" If Eve was going to think differently, it would require her to change the way she looked at her illness and her anger with God.

As I talked with Eve, we discussed that choice and turned to Paul's letter to the Romans. Here Paul defines the best way that any of us can look at life's problems and grow from them.

And we know that God causes all things to work together for good to those who love God, to those who are called according to His purpose. For those whom He foreknew, He also predestined to become conformed to the image of His Son, so that He would be the firstborn among many brethren . . .

—Romans 8:28–29

Deciding What the Problem Is

Understanding those fifty-four short words would lay the foundation for Eve to *change her mind* (repent) about her anger. Until we talked, Eve had been dealing with her illness according to the way she felt, and most of the time she did not feel good. Her strong negative emotions colored her thinking. But instead of living and dying in an emotional swamp, Paul called her to conduct her life differently through his first three words, "And we know." For a year Eve *knew* her life was terrible and that knowledge—that interpretation—shaped all of her responses. Instead, we agreed that she had to change what she "knew" about things.

Eve believed that God had abandoned or afflicted her because of something she had done. Even worse, she thought that maybe God just did not care about her trouble. The things she *thought* she knew were causing most of her trouble—and they were wrong.

So Paul's word to her was, "God causes all things to work for good." Immediately, what she "knew" changed. *God causes*! If God causes, he must be directly involved in the process. That meant that the moment she fell ill, through all the days in the hospital, she was never alone or out of God's care. A paragraph later, Paul emphasized the point when he asks, "What shall separate us from the love of God?" and answers by saying that *nothing* can separate us from God's love.

So everything that happened to Eve is included in the phrase "all things." All things—good, bad, or indifferent—are part of God's purpose for our lives. Nothing is left out or left to chance.

It is important to understand what God is "causing" in these verses. Paul is not telling us that God is just causing all things, but that God causes *all things to work together for our good.* God takes our success and failure, our illness and health, and everything else, whether good or bad, and uses it for our *good*. This put Eve's illness in a completely different light. She had considered it awful then, but now she needed to *change her mind* and see it as God did, something he would use for her good.

As Eve and I continued through the verse, we came next to "those who love God, to those called according his purpose." The whole idea that I can change how I think about things is wrapped up in those two words, "love God." It is linked to the question Jesus asked Martha: "Do you believe this?"

Seeing Disaster as God Sees It

The ability to see disaster within a framework that is *good* requires us to love God more than the things we lose. This means I must know him, believe him, and trust him. In the amazing conversation in the Upper Room, Jesus connected these two concepts and added a third. He started by telling the eleven, "Do not let your heart be troubled; believe in God, believe also in Me" (John 14:1). When he told them he was leaving (for the cross), Thomas wanted to know where he was going and Jesus responded, "I am the way, and the truth, and the life, no one comes to the Father but through me" (John 14:6). Further, Jesus tells them that if they loved him, they would keep his commandments (John 14:15).

The connection is striking. We know, believe, love, trust, and obey Jesus. When it comes to dealing with sadness caused by loss, the non-Christian is at an incredible disadvantage because he cannot believe and love someone he does not know.[5]

When we know God loving him allows us the choice to see our "catastrophe" as his tool. We know that God loves us and that he is all-wise, so we know that whatever he allows into our lives will be for our good and his glory. While we might not be able to see or understand it at the time, we can trust like Martha did. Martha

---

[5]It is important for all of us to understand this point. For those who want more information, please see Appendix A.

believed and trusted Jesus even if Lazarus had to stay in the grave until Christ's second coming.

We can depend on God the same way. We know that whatever we lose, God intends to use that loss well and wisely. Eve's illness took on a completely different meaning when she could see God rearranging her life. That dulled a lot of the pain associated with the losses. They became, as Paul said, lost things he could now count as a gain because of the way God used them (see Phil. 3:7).

Loving God More than Things

This required Eve to internalize the words that came after "love God." She had to become a person who acknowledged that she was "called according to *his* purpose." The emphasis on his purpose is very important because we can so easily substitute what *we* think is good for us. Eve had lived under the false assumption that her goals in life were God's goals. She saw them as essentially good things that she was being denied because of the disease.

Wanting them was not wrong in itself, but when getting them became the most important thing in her life, it set the stage for Eve's tumble into anger. Eve could believe that God was denying her these things for his own amusement, or she could believe that God was telling her "no" to accomplish his purpose for her life. And perhaps he was telling her no for her own good.

I grew up in a church with people who loved Romans 8:28, or at least part of it. "All things work together for good!" We would smile and say that to people whose lives looked like a crater from a 1000-pound bomb. Most of the time they wanted to kill us on the spot! I suspect that most of us never learned the rest of the verse until much later in life. I know that none of us really grasped the significance of verse 29.

The purpose for Eve's suffering was in verse 29: "For those whom He foreknew, He also predestined *to become* conformed to the image of His Son." The purpose God had in mind all along was for Eve to become more like Christ. Eve needed to be sick! Her life was going to be changed by that illness. The sooner she figured that out, the sooner she could quit being angry with God over it.

Repenting of Anger, Finding the Purpose

Eve repented of that anger. Instead of sinfully accusing God of neglecting her, Eve needed to keep in mind that sadness was a time to ask two important questions. A good friend taught me this when I was having a bad day. He told me to ask myself, "Why has the sovereign God of the universe let this come into my life now? What does God want to change about me to make me more like Christ?"[6]

After she asked herself those questions, Eve asked God to open her heart to whatever message he had for her in the trouble she was facing. Instead of becoming angry because she was denied something she wanted badly, Eve examined that desire in light of God's Word, so that she could find a response that pleased God. She also had a circle of friends she could call on to help her in the process.

When she identified what she thought God might want her to change, Eve made a plan to make the changes. She also agreed to apply Scripture to her emotional responses. Instead of staying sad or angry about her problem, Eve sought to apply what the apostle James said and count her trial "all joy" (James 1:2–5). She could have the same joy Jesus did as he went to the cross (Heb. 12:2). It would be joy born out of the change God would bring to her life through her problem.

Eve pursued the following pattern of behavior every day and it freed her from the anger:

1. Sadness over loss would be her cue to consider her problem and her attitude the way James directs. She would move her thinking to the place where she could count the problem as joy. She would ask herself the Why and What questions my friend shared with me.

2. She would ask God to open her heart to the things that needed to change.

---

[6]Randy Patten, the Executive Director of National Association of Nouthetic Counselors, gave me these questions along with other very good biblical counsel when I was dealing with a significant problem.

3. Eve would examine her situation according to Scripture to find the best biblical response to her problem.

4. She would make a plan to change her behavior and attitude so that she could count the trial as joy and implement the changes. She would ask God for the power from his grace to make the changes and thank him for the chance to change.

In time Eve learned to respond to loss and change with the joy of knowing that God could use them as opportunities for growth. There were many things in Eve's life that God could change in this process.

Sadness as a Signal Instead of Disease

Anyone who deals with sadness and sorrow can benefit from Eve's experience. Sadness can be a great gift. It allows us to look into our hearts and see if there is something closer to us than the God we love. It is the cue that tells us it is time to consider and adjust our thinking so that we can say without reservation that we want to glorify God with our lives more than we want to breathe. It gives us the opportunity to identify the things we worship more than God and repent of them.

Prolonged sadness that descends into prodigal living requires repentance. Perhaps it is better to say that when we come to our senses, we have the privilege of confessing and forsaking sin. When our sadness is caused by our sin or our sinful response to trials, it can result in a depressed mood that is often labeled as the disease depression. But repentance can be the tool to escape the dark mood.

Eve struggled with a lot more than anger. She had become an expert in fear and worry. Eve would learn that fear and worry were just as much sins against God as her anger and ingratitude. These were the next items on the list of things that things that could change with repentance.

12

Worry: Another Door to Sadness

Eve had become a habitually angry person, and she also had become really good at worrying. Her fear of a relapse had made her an expert at the art of fretting. Although it is not used much these days, "fretting" is a great word. Webster's says it means "to become vexed or worried."[1] It came to us from a Middle English word, fretan, which meant "to devour."

When the King James translators chose the word "fret" for Psalm 37, they were apparently looking for a word to describe being virtually eaten alive by emotion. Later translators would use it as well.

Do not fret because of evildoers,
Be not envious toward wrongdoers.
For they will wither quickly like the grass
And fade like the green herb.
Trust in the LORD and do good;
Dwell in the land and cultivate faithfulness.
Delight yourself in the LORD;
And He will give you the desires of your heart.
Commit your way to the LORD,

---

[1] Webster's online dictionary, http://www.merriam-webster.com/dictionary/fret (6/3/2012).

Trust also in Him, and He will do it.
He will bring forth your righteousness as the light
And your judgment as the noonday.
Rest in the LORD and wait patiently for Him;
Do not fret because of him who prospers in his way,
Because of the man who carries out wicked schemes.
Cease from anger and forsake wrath;
Do not fret; it leads only to evildoing.

—Psalm 37:1–8

The psalmist urges us not to be eaten up by envy towards those who have what we want. It's a lot like Miss Havisham in Charles Dickens's *Great Expectations*. She spent her whole life in the wedding dress she wore on the day she was left at the altar by her beloved fiancé. She spent all her time thinking about how to get even with men, including using Estella to break Pip's heart. In the end, her dress catches fire and she dies as a result. Miss Havisham was a world-class fretter and it consumed her!

The warning at the end of the psalm is echoed in *Great Expectations*: "Do not fret; it leads only to evildoing." Eve's fretting had led to much "evildoing." Now she needed to learn how to stop the repetitive, useless rumination about her illness and the losses she sustained as a result.

If unresolved sadness and anger are doorways into the dark garden of a depressed mood, then worry is the fertilizer that makes it grow. Many medicines prescribed for depression today are also prescribed for the treatment of anxiety. Most people today view it as a disease, but anxiety is just another word for what the Bible describes as worry. There isn't a person on earth who is unfamiliar with the symptoms.

The parents who watch the clock, wondering where their child is after 11 p.m.; the student waiting as the teacher hands out the final exam; and the husband who wonders how he will make the house payment if his job is eliminated—they all understand worry. Sixty to 90 percent of people diagnosed with depression are diagnosed with anxiety as well.[2] For Eve, worry helped keep the consuming fire of sadness and anger burning. This was another thing Eve needed to reconsider.

Changing the Anxious Mind

For Eve, worry was an adverse emotion like sadness. It could lead either to an opportunity to reconsider/repent or it could lead to deadly thinking and behavior like the sorrow of the world. The best place in Scripture to help her reconsider worry was Jesus' words about it in Matthew's gospel.

> "For this reason I say to you, do not be worried about your life, as to what you will eat or what you will drink; nor for your body, as to what you will put on. Is not life more than food, and the body more than clothing? Look at the birds of the air, that they do not sow, nor reap nor gather into barns, and yet your heavenly Father feeds them. Are you not worth much more than they? And who of you by being worried can add a single hour to his life? And why are you worried about clothing? Observe how the lilies of the field grow; they do not toil nor do they spin, yet I say to you that not even Solomon in all his glory clothed himself like one of these. But if God so clothes the grass of the field, which is alive today and tomorrow is thrown into the furnace, will He not much more clothe you? You of little faith! Do not worry then, saying, 'What will we eat?' or 'What will we drink?' or 'What will we wear for clothing?' For the Gentiles eagerly seek all these things; for your heavenly Father knows that you need all these things. But seek first His kingdom and His righteousness, and all these things will be added to you. So do not worry about tomorrow; for tomorrow will care for itself. Each day has enough trouble of its own."
>
> —Matthew 6:25–34

From the lips of God to our ears comes the best description of worry in print. It described Eve. She worried about everything Jesus talked about: life, position, possessions. The good news came

---

[2] Healthyplace.com on 1/2/2012. http://www.healthyplace.com/depression/main/relationship-between-depression-and-anxiety/menu-id-68/.

when Jesus said three times for emphasis, "Do not worry." The grammar is the same in Greek and English. "Do not worry" is an imperative—a command. It is a command God intends us to obey, by his grace and the power of the indwelling Holy Spirit.

Eve was not in the grip of a mental disease. Eve just had things she had made more important than her worship of God. Health, wealth, position, husband, and children had all become objects of her idolatrous worship. And when she faced their possible loss, she was consumed by worry about how to get them back. Yet the fact that this was idolatry was actually good news!

It was good news to a woman drowning in worry and the behavior that resulted. Why? Because as long as Eve could agree that Christ had described her worry as disobedience, then she could repent, find forgiveness for her sin, change her mind, and change her behavior. To do that, I directed her to a letter Paul wrote while imprisoned at Philippi.

The fact that Paul wrote the letter from jail was very important to Eve. She might dismiss what I told her about worry. She could look me in the eye and say what I have heard often in counseling. "You have everything I want. It's easy for you to say I shouldn't worry!" But this letter was written by a man sitting in jail, who had lost everything most of us consider important.

> But whatever things were gain to me, those things I have counted as loss for the sake of Christ. More than that, I count all things to be loss in view of the surpassing value of knowing Christ Jesus my Lord, for whom I have suffered the loss of all things, and count them but rubbish so that I may gain Christ.
> —Philippians 3:7–8

Knowing Jesus Christ as his Lord and Savior was more important to Paul than everything he lost when he chose to follow him. So Paul could sit in jail, write the letter to the Christians at Philippi and mean every word of it.

> Rejoice in the Lord always; again I will say, rejoice! Let your gentle spirit be known to all men. The Lord is near. Be anxious for noth-

ing, but in everything by prayer and supplication with thanksgiving let your requests be made known to God. And the peace of God, which surpasses all comprehension, will guard your hearts and your minds in Christ Jesus. Finally, brethren, whatever is true, whatever is honorable, whatever is right, whatever is pure, whatever is lovely, whatever is of good repute, if there is any excellence and if anything worthy of praise, dwell on these things. The things you have learned and received and heard and seen in me, practice these things, and the God of peace will be with you.

—Philippians 4:4–9

Eve read those verses and allowed God to change her heart.

Changing My Mind, Choosing to Rejoice

Was it unreasonable for Paul to tell Eve to "Rejoice in the Lord always; again I will say rejoice!"? That might not be the thing I tell someone in the middle of a new struggle, but Eve's problem wasn't new. She had been at this for months and when she came to talk, she was looking for direction.

Eve did not cause her problem, but over time she was responsible for the way she chose to respond to it. In order for Eve to have joy like Hannah, she had to change the way she looked at her trial. She knew that changing her perspective would be a major part of the solution God had for her. Instead of fearfully worrying about the things she had lost, Eve now chose to be grateful for the things God allowed her to have.

Choosing to Act Biblically

As Eve was repenting and changing her mind about worry and joy, she also knew that the change had to be applied to the way she treated others as she worried. "Let your gentle spirit be evident to all men. The Lord is near." It was not hard to be unkind when she was preoccupied with worry, but instead, Eve was called to be kind and gentle.

Eve struggled with Paul's admonitions, "Don't worry!" "Be anxious for nothing." She might have been tempted not to even try, but she had learned that if God was telling her not to worry, he intended to enable her to obey by his grace.

Asking for a Better Solution

The rest of the passage was equally helpful. "In everything by prayer and supplication with thanksgiving let your requests be made known to God." At a time in my life when I was struggling with worry, I decided that Paul must have meant that I could ask God for a better solution to the problem I was facing. Eve could ask God for a better solution just like I did, as have countless other believers.

I told Eve that I believed I could ask God for a better answer to my problem because Jesus did the same thing in the garden of Gethsemane. "And He went a little beyond them, and fell on His face and prayed, saying, 'My Father, if it is possible, let this cup pass from Me; yet not as I will, but as You will'" (Matt. 26: 39).

Jesus asked for a better solution but then told his Father that he would drink the cup God had for him. Eve knew she could ask God for a better solution. At the same time, she knew God could decide that the best solution was for her to continue in the problem. She was willing to accept this as Jesus did. If nothing could change, she would be thankful for the grace God would give her to go through it.

There was an extra blessing for Eve as she submitted to God by thanking him for the problem when asking for a solution. She got peace! She received the peace that comes from knowing that the God who loved her is in charge of the outcome. She had peace because she put herself in his hands. That gave her the "peace of God that surpasses all comprehension," as Paul said in verse 7. She knew she could not fix the problem. She knew it was in the hands of the God who could or who had a better solution.

That still left her struggling a bit and drifting back to worry, but Eve found help in the next verse. Paul told Eve and all who worry to think about things that are true, honorable, right, pure, lovely, of good repute, excellent, and praiseworthy. When Eve drifted back to worry, she remembered those words and another very important thing.

Beloved

Eve exchanged her worry, fear, and anger for peace, but eventually she found that there was more to life than just getting out of the frying pan and the fire. Eve's relationship to the God she trusted for salvation needed something. She needed to understand it better. If she was going to avoid being pulled back into the downward spiral of worry, fear, anger, and sadness, she needed to know that she was "beloved."[3]

I pointed Eve to Paul's words to the Ephesians.

> Therefore be imitators of God, as beloved children; and walk in love, just as Christ also loved you and gave Himself up for us, an offering and a sacrifice to God as a fragrant aroma. But immorality or any impurity or greed must not even be named among you, as is proper among saints . . .
>
> —Ephesians 5:1–3

The key to Paul's words is "beloved." Without it, nothing else in his statement will ever happen. Unless Eve believed that she was God's beloved, she would not imitate God or walk in love or give herself up for others. All that would be left to her would be immorality, impurity, and greed. Eve had been greedy for all the things she could not have because of her illness. Now it was time for her to live as a beloved child.

This required Eve to believe that God did not have her on a "performance contract." In reality she was beloved if she did well and she was beloved if she did poorly. We are beloved because we are in Christ (see Rom. 8:1 and John 17:17–21). When God looked at Eve, he did not see her good or bad behavior. He saw Jesus and, as he said at Christ's baptism, "This is my beloved Son, in Whom I am well-pleased" (Matt. 3:17). When Eve understood that, it

---

[3]Elyse Fitpatrick, *Because He Loves Me* (Wheaton, Ill.: Crossway, 2008). I am indebted to Elyse Fitzpatrick and this book for forcing me to enjoy this concept!

made her smile. Eve knew that she was a sinner, as we all are. But when God looked at her, "beloved" and "well-pleased" were the words that came to God's mind. Eve was not merely tolerated or put up with by God. God loved her!

Escaping Performance Contract Christianity

When we believe that we relate to God through "performance-contract Christianity," we hold everyone else to the same miserable contract. If you perform well, I will love you. If you do not, I will withhold that love. In its place go worry, fear, anger, and often a sad mood. We will do this with people and we will do it with God. If God does not perform according to our expectations, we can even start talking about the necessity of being "honestly" angry with God. The real solution is to repent before God, receive his forgiveness, and more truly understand our relationship to God.

We do not serve God to gain his favor or to get things from him. We serve God because he first loved us and we now love him. This thought changed a lot of things for Eve. Instead of being angry with God because of the loss she suffered, she had peace with God because she knew he loved her and had a plan for her problem. Knowing this, she could give up her worrying.

Eve had been completely focused on herself and her own comfort. Now she could live the way Paul taught the Ephesians. As a beloved child, she could imitate Jesus (in his strength) and serve others. This took her mind away from her own problems and towards serving God and others. This was the ultimate solution to her anger, worry, and sad mood. For the 90 percent of Americans labeled with depression whose sadness actually stems from loss, it offers the same hope.

13

Choosing Good Moods over Bad

I n the area of emotional well-being, life in the United States has been changing since 1950 and accelerating every year. The list of things that could contribute to our troubled moods is lengthy. It would be hard to pin down one cause for it all, but change in the arena of faith seems very significant.

Depression has become a very different thing than it was before 1950. People born before 1950 had a much lower rate of depression than those born after that year. Out of those born before 1955, only 1 percent would have a major depressive episode before age seventy-five. Among those born after 1955, 6 percent would have a major depressive episode by age twenty-five. In some parts of the world, the younger generation was three times more likely to be diagnosed with depression than the older.[1] That's the bad news. The good news is that we've seen that there is a way out of this.

There are lots of explanations for the rise in depression diagnoses, but it makes me wonder why my parents, grandparents, and great-grandparents could suffer through multiple world wars and

---

[1]Daniel Goleman, "A Rising Cost of Modernity: Depression," *New York Times,* Dec. 8, 1992, www.nytimes.com, (1/27/2012).

unprecedented economic depression without getting depressed. This book has attempted to make a good case for the idea that today, people in medicine, psychology, and society in general mistake sadness for depression. This alone could account for a significant portion of the increase in our mood disorders.

Another explanation also deserves consideration. While we are mislabeling sadness as depression, it is also possible that we have lost our ability to respond to sadness in a way that turns it into a productive emotion which drives useful change. Researchers suggest that the changes in our families over the last fifty years have left us more vulnerable and less supported when difficult times come.

Martin Seligman came closest to the truth when he said:

One cause of depression is a tendency to magnify the effects of setbacks. . . . To the extent you see a failure as something that is lasting and which you magnify to taint everything in your life, you are prone to let a momentary defeat become a lasting sense of hopelessness. . . . But if you have a larger perspective, like a belief in God and an afterlife, and you lose your job, it's just a temporary defeat. You know that justice will prevail in the long run and you don't plummet into depression.[2]

That is what we have lost as a nation and (in part) as the church over the last fifty years. Our nation grows more secular every minute. As we drift away from the things our grandparents knew and our forefathers believed, we have lost the assurance that our current setbacks are temporary and our future eternal.

As our churches have sought to become more user-friendly to an increasingly secular and materialistic world, I wonder if we have lost the ability to sing songs that say this world is not our home. Have we grown so comfortable trying to make "heaven on earth" that we don't know what to do when unhappy events rob us of our creature comforts?

---

[2]Goleman, *A Rising Cost of Modernity:Depression,* ibid.

There is a solution to the rising tide of bad moods for individuals and even whole societies. We can see it in the different paths that Susan and Eve took to deal with their really bad moods.

A Nation Looking for a Cure

Americans today are far more receptive to the idea that depressed moods come from disease than they were in 1950. Susan and Eve walked the pathway that has become common in American life. The idea that anyone who is sad for more than two weeks may suffer from a mood disorder is now as American as apple pie. We are bombarded with this message on a daily basis. We are told that it is not reasonable for anyone to suffer sadness. It is viewed as needless pain.

Television commercials for many medications promise to turn our black and white sadness into living-color joy. Relatives and neighbors tell us we need something to stabilize our emotions. Most who struggle with sadness will look for a medical solution. In our society, this is a reasonable expectation. The problem is that 90 percent do not seem to benefit.

Instead, they remind us of the woman in Luke who pursued the best health care available but got no better. Ninety percent of those who pursue better moods medically gain nothing but diagnostic labels.

Remembering the Value of Sadness

Susan and Eve give us a reason to reconsider the value we place on the sadness that all of us will experience. If we look at sorrow and decide, as many do today, that there is no real value in living through it, we stand to lose so much. We lose an integral part of our created being, designed by God to move us in his direction.

Susan and Eve both suffered a loss and both were grieved by it. Susan suffered pain and lost her sense of well-being. Eve suffered physical pain and lost six months of her life. Both struggled with sadness, fear, worry, anger, and a depressed mood. They illustrate two very different ways to interpret and deal with loss and sadness. Their grief took them in very different directions.

Susan's physical pain led to a diagnosis of depression and then bipolar disorder. Susan experienced the care one can now expect to receive, when her physician decides that her physical and emotional distress is due to depression, anxiety, or bipolar disorder.[3] It becomes a medical problem to be solved by medical treatment.

Eve struggled her way through anxiety and depression, complicated by drunkenness. I do not know why she chose to come to the counseling center where I met with her. But with that choice she took a different path from Susan. Instead of being labeled depressed and bipolar, Eve simply was not labeled. When she told me she thought she was depressed, I acknowledged what she said. When she said that she thought we could talk about it eventually, I agreed. But I did not give her a label and we did not talk about it until the last visit.

Being labeled has its own set of difficulties. It makes a person feel as if he is a victim of disease. The label (or rather the diagnosis) means that the bearer is ill and cannot recover without help. The label means that I must depend on someone else to fix me.

Embracing Sadness and Avoiding Labels

The biggest problem with labeling is that we quit looking for an answer. Once we have the label, we have the answer. The label determines how we respond to our problem. It drives our thinking, emotions, and behavior. Susan suffered through this until she decided that five years was enough to devote to a label without a cure. The diagnosis of depression may lead to additional labels such as bipolar disorder if no cure can be found. If we choose to deal with sadness and suffering this way, it seems only to lead to more problems.

There is good news in all this. Eve found her way out of her sadness years before Susan did because a label did not keep her from

---

[3] A discussion of bipolar disorder as currently diagnosed and treated follows in chapters 14 and 15.

considering a different explanation for her problem. Eve understood what Susan would learn later—that trouble and sorrow have great value when we pursue it guided by 2 Corinthians 7:10. When we choose to see sorrow the way God intends, we do not sorrow as those who have no hope. Godly sorrow leads to changes in our mind's perspective and our heart's priorities. The sorrow of the world often leads to deadly detours in living.

"Jesus Knows All About Our Struggles"[4]

At the heart of this good news is the message that Martha and Mary received. Jesus knows about our sorrows and he weeps with us. When the children of Israel suffered under Pharaoh, the Bible says that God saw it and cared.

> So God heard their groaning; and God remembered His covenant with Abraham, Isaac, and Jacob. God saw the sons of Israel, and God took notice of them.
>
> —Exodus 2:24–25

When we sorrow over losses, God knows it and has a plan for it just as he had a plan for Lazarus. That plan for our sorrow will always be better than any solution we can devise. As Joseph told his brothers, who were the cause of at least two decades of trial and separation from his family, "As for you, you meant evil against me, but God meant it for good in order to bring about this present result, to preserve many people alive" (Gen. 50:20).

God intends to take our sorrow and change us through it by his grace, just as he changed Hannah. A woman who sorrowed over her childlessness became a woman who gave her son to serve God in the temple. Hannah is an illustration of what godly sorrowing can do in our lives. Hannah and Joseph are Old Testament pictures that bring to life Paul's words in Romans 8:28–29. They lost and

---

[4]Words from the chorus of the hymn by Johnson Oatman Jr., "There's not a friend like the lowly Jesus, No not one, No not one!" *Worship and Service Hymnal* (Carol Stream, Ill.: Hope Publishing, 1976), 236.

sorrowed. They grew and changed. God was glorified and great good came from it.

Our Genes Do Not Decide Who We Can Become

The very idea that we can change is good news. Our label-oriented society is struggling under the medical impression that once we are diagnosed with a mood disorder, our brains (and our lives) will never change unless medically altered. It is good to know from recent science that our brains can change in response to our thoughts and actions.

It should have come as no surprise that Eve and Susan could change. The Bible has many passages to support the idea. As Paul said to the church at Corinth, "Therefore if anyone is in Christ, he is a new creature; the old things passed away; behold, new things have come" (2 Cor. 5:17).

The idea that believers could "put off" old bad habits (sins) and "put on" godly behavior (Eph. 4:22–24) is so vital to Christian theology that denying it leaves the gospel impotent. So Paul would tell us again in his letter to the Corinthians:

> Or do you not know that the unrighteous will not inherit the king-dom of God? Do not be deceived; neither fornicators, nor idolaters, nor adulterers, nor effeminate, nor homosexuals, nor thieves, nor the covetous, nor drunkards, nor revilers, nor swindlers, will inherit the kingdom of God. *Such were some of you*; but you were washed, but you were sanctified, but you were justified in the name of the Lord Jesus Christ and in the Spirit of our God.
>
> —1 Corinthians 6:9–11 [author's emphasis]

Orthodox Christianity has never agreed that we are doomed to continue the same unprofitable behavior for a lifetime because of our genetics. The Bible clearly says what Susan and Eve discovered: When they responded to their sadness and reconsidered what they were thinking and doing, they could change.

Leaving the Graveyard

Like Martha and Mary, Eve and Susan both had their own graveyard moments. After Jesus wept, he said, "Roll away the stone"
(John 11:39) and they did. Grief over Lazarus was the beginning
of amazing change. The dead man would live. When Eve and Susan
concluded that there was no purpose in their sadness any longer,
they reconsidered their situation and, with God's help, changed
their hearts and minds.

Allowing sadness to lead us to change is not something we are
left to do on our own. The change starts in our hearts when we
abandon self-interest as the driving force behind our actions and
emotions (see James 4:1–4). In the life of the Christian, this change
is powered by God's grace. We are saved by grace, and we live by
grace. We are his workmanship and not our own (Eph. 2:8–9).

It was God who acted "so that as Christ was raised from the
dead through the glory of the Father, so we too might walk in
newness of life" (Rom. 6:4). When Jesus told Martha and Mary
to have the stone removed, they did it, but it was Jesus who raised
Lazarus from the dead. In the same way, when we respond to our
losses and sadness by leading our thinking to "consider it all joy,"
we can grow and mature in Christ. And we can avoid complicating
the difficult situations in life with our sin.

When we do respond badly as believers, we are privileged to
repent, confess our sin, and find forgiveness. In the process of
changing our thinking and our behavior, it is God who graciously
empowers us to do it.

Given the Choice

I'm not sure I can say that America is at a crossroads today. I think
we made that choice in the 1960s when we set our national policy
away from Christianity toward secularism. That choice has been
reinforced with thousands of choices since then and it has redefined
how Americans interpret loss, suffering, and sorrow. However, we
do have a couple of choices left.

If you have read this far but are not a believer in Christ, I encourage you to read Appendix A. There you will learn how to find the same gift I found at age nineteen. It is the first step on a path that will lead you to consider what sadness, sorrow, and loss really mean.

If you know Christ and are struggling with loss and sadness, there is real hope in seeing sorrow the way Paul did. Godly sorrow that leads to repentance leads to hope. The ultimate hope we have as believers is seen in a letter that John wrote to the church.

> See how great a love the Father has bestowed on us, that we would be called children of God; and such we are. For this reason the world does not know us, because it did not know Him. Beloved, now we are children of God, and it has not appeared as yet what we will be. We know that when He appears, we will be like Him, because we will see Him just as He is. And everyone who has this hope fixed on Him purifies himself, just as He is pure.
>
> —1 John 3:1–3

In these words we see that anyone who trusts in Christ will ultimately see him and be like him. In the meantime, our sadness can remind us to be about his business, loving him and others, serving him and others, and purifying ourselves as he is pure. It calls us to consider what God wants to do in our lives so that we can grow and become more like our Savior. Our sadness calls us to the same joy our Savior had as he thought about rescuing us from the penalty for our sin.

As Christians, we have a choice in the way we deal with trials that cause us sorrow. We can become victims of the struggle or we can choose to honor God and grow. It is my hope that you will choose to use sorrow in a godly way that leads to a life that glorifies and honors our loving, faithful, and magnificent God.

14

The Link Between Depression and Bipolar Disorder

When I set out to write this book, I intended to write about bipolar disorder. It is a subject I often speak about. In counseling and in medicine, there seems to be a noticeable increase in the number of people described as bipolar. The disorder is becoming a concern in counseling because the diagnosis is being presented by troubled individuals as the cause of their behavior.

The problems this presents are similar to those that arise when people are diagnosed with depression. People are seen as victims of a disease when the diagnosis was made solely by observing behavior. To sort this out, I decided that I needed to understand what bipolar disorder was, what causes it, and what I can do about it for the people I counsel and for whom I provide medical care. As is sometimes the case, when we start peeling back the layers of a problem, we discover that the real issue is not the problem we originally set out to understand.

This was true for me with bipolar disorder. The longer I looked at it, the less it seemed to be the root issue. The true source of the problem lay elsewhere. The real reason for the surge in bipolar disorder diagnoses was not the fact that we had a new disease or that we were in the grip of an epidemic of an old one. Instead, the problem seemed rooted in the way we diagnose and treat depression today.

As this book has sought to explain, the diagnosis of depression is based on a medical professional's subjective assessment of a patient, using criteria prescribed by the Diagnostic and Statistical Manual of Mental Disorders (DSM). In other words, it is a matter of professional opinion to a large extent. As we have seen, the criteria used to make the diagnosis are insufficiently precise, and thus tend to label as depressed large numbers of people who are simply sad over a loss. Because the diagnosis of depression lacks laboratory or x-ray testing that can validate it, growing numbers of people who struggle with their moods are labeled depressed.

When they go to their doctors for help, they are given medications that often have significant side effects. If they fail to improve, more medications are added and with them come more side effects. This is the aspect of depression that caught my attention a decade ago. In it is also the explanation for the increase in and evolution of bipolar disorder.

Today we diagnose bipolar disorder with the same method and criteria we use for depression. The symptoms of the disorder have been described in the DSM so that any observer can reliably identify individuals who may have the problem. Unfortunately, like depression, there are no good laboratory or x-ray tests that can confirm the diagnosis. Once again we are left with a diagnosis that is largely a matter of opinion, not objective findings. To sort this out, we need to understand what those criteria are and how we got them.

What Is Bipolar Disorder?

I saw bipolar disorder for the first time as a medical student in 1972. It was then called manic depression. To qualify for this diagnosis, a patient had to meet certain criteria. During my junior year psychiatry rotation, I encountered one such patient, a salesman who was interviewed for the benefit of the medical students.

In the first interview, he seemed to be the life of the party. He talked rapidly, telling jokes. Most of us thought he should have been a stand-up comedian. We did not understand what was wrong with him. He seemed to need to talk very fast, as if he were afraid he might not be allowed to finish his sentences. The man stated that he did not need much sleep and, in fact, had not slept for days. What he did need was to get out of the hospital so that he could get back to work. He had some important business deals to conclude that would bring him a considerable fortune. His hospitalization was jeopardizing his business, and he hoped that the physician interviewing him would sign his discharge that morning.

The next session occurred some time later and revealed a startling change in the salesman's behavior. It was hard to believe that he was the same man. There were no jokes or mentions of business deals. It seemed as if someone or something had taken all the fire out of his engine. His speech was slow and he looked a little like he was in a fog. He seemed embarrassed when asked about the big deals and fortunes he had mentioned earlier. Now he looked like a man suffering from profound hypothyroidism. He had no energy.

Between the first and second interview, the man had been given lithium, which was (and still is) a common medicine used to treat manic depression. He was now sleeping normally and was no longer making ruinous financial deals. He was in the hospital because his family was trying to protect him and themselves from financial ruin. They succeeded, but as medical students we wondered whether what was left of the man was a cure or another problem.

In a discussion session that followed, we told the psychiatrist our opinion of the cure. The psychiatrist listened patiently to our inexperienced viewpoint and then agreed with us. Yes, the man was a lot more fun to watch when he was flying high in the clouds of delusions of grandeur. But it wasn't any fun for him. We were told that patients like our salesman report being terrified by the manic phase. To them it was like riding in a car on a crowded street at a hundred miles an hour with no brakes or steering wheel. That's why the salesman felt better on his medicine. The challenge for the family, patient, and psychiatrist was to keep him on his medication. Even though he supposedly felt better taking it, the medication did have side effects and he would most likely stop taking it in a few months, as he had in the past.

Manic Depression Becomes Bipolar Disorder I

The salesman's symptoms were a good example of what is now called bipolar disorder I. At that time, mania was treated with lithium or antipsychotic medications and the depression that followed was treated with antidepressants.[1] The antidepressants available at that time had significant side effects and some potential to trigger mania in certain individuals. This meant that most patients would be treated not by family physicians, but by psychiatrists. I think most of us as young physicians were relieved by that.

As a result, I saw very little of manic depression over the next twenty years. During that time, the prevalence of manic depression was considered to be about 0.1 percent of the population, which meant that there would have been roughly 250,000 individuals in the entire country needing lithium and laboratory testing.[2] In the state of Indiana, where I practice, there might have been six thousand patients at any given time diagnosed with manic depression. In the Indianapolis area, with a population of nearly a million at the time, that would translate to about a thousand patients. There were ample numbers of psychiatrists to provide their care. Had nothing changed, there would have been no reason for me to write on the subject today.

But things did change. In 1995, I encountered the first of a new kind of manic depressive. By then, manic depression had been renamed bipolar disorder and was in the process of changing even more.

---

[1] David Healy, "The Latest Mania: Selling Bipolar Disorder," *PLoS Medicine*, Vol.3, 4, (April 2006) 2. PLoS Medicine is the online medical journal of the Public Library of Science and can be found at www.plosmedicine.org .
[2] Ibid., 4.

Considering the Symptoms

The young lady who continued my medical education on this subject was a single mother who had come to see me for medical care. She had two small children who had been labeled with attention deficit hyperactivity disorder and were doing poorly with the prescribed treatment. Their problems in school and their behavior at home were straining the limits of a woman who was working forty hours a week and then coming home to the full-time job of keeping a house and raising children.

She simply could not cope with all this alone. Her husband had long gone and was no help to her. She was also seeing a psychiatrist and being treated for depression. Unfortunately, her depression failed to respond to any of the medications he gave her. Her psychiatrist then decided that because she was not responding to the treatment, she must have another problem. Soon she was labeled as bipolar.

According to the criteria then being applied, bipolar behavior:

- Includes a period lasting more than one week during which individuals are in a better mood than usual.
- Patients can be irritable, with an inflated sense of self-esteem, a decreased need for sleep, racing thoughts and a need to talk a lot.
- Patients may be easily distracted, expressing an increased need to get things done.
- Patients often spend money they do not have and may make disastrous sexual and moral choices.

The period of mania is usually followed by a period of depression.[3]

I mentally inventoried the symptoms associated with manic depression and found that this patient just did not seem to have them. She did not stay up all night. She was not spending recklessly. Apart from her unfortunate marriage, she was not making

---

[3]Bipolar Disorder: Epidemiology and Diagnosis, UpToDate Online 16.3. Retrieved electronically on 3/18/09 at www.uptodate.com .

disastrous sexual choices. The other strange thing was that she was not taking lithium. Instead, she had been given a medication usually reserved for the treatment of seizures.

Whatever disease this patient had, it did not seem to have anything to do with manic depression. What's more, the medication she was taking did not seem to help her. I was convinced of the reality of manic depression by the things I saw in 1972, but nothing in this patient's life looked anything like the salesman. That day I simply saw a young woman overwhelmed by the demands of caring for her family. As I said earlier, she had been abandoned by her husband and had no other help. She was not a Christian and had no spiritual framework to help her deal with her struggles. On top of that, she was being given medications with significant side effects that did not seem to help.

The young mother's story was a lot like Susan's, in that both of them ended up in a disease category that was relatively new. Both ended up with a revised diagnosis that was just as subjective as their earlier diagnosis of depression. Neither of them was like the salesman I saw in 1972, which raised some questions for me. The first was: How did we get from manic depression to bipolar disorder?

Getting from MD to BPD

The history of manic depression and bipolar disorder is a complicated one. As we said earlier, it is complicated because for the last 200 years the diagnosis of mental disorders has been largely a matter of professional opinion. And there have been lots of opinions that have given us names like circular insanity, cycloid psychosis, and folie circulaire.[4] Without objective evidence such as laboratory, x-ray, or even physical exam findings, the diagnosis of bipolar disorder was made using a history of the patient's behavior and family.

This should not come as a surprise since the whole of medicine had for centuries been governed more by opinion than fact. When Hippocrates and his Greek colleagues decided that disease

---

[4]For an excellent history of the diagnosis of mania, see *Mania: A Short History of Bipolar Disorder*, by David Healy (Baltimore: Johns Hopkins Press, 2008).

was caused by an imbalance in our "humors," they did so because they simply did not know any better. Medicine was mostly art with little, if any, science involved. When physicians encountered the plague, they killed the cats, not realizing that it was actually the rats the cats ate that carried the fleas that carried the disease. They meant well, but they worsened the problem.

But hope was coming. In 1900, medicine as a profession was on the brink of a revolution and every branch, including psychiatry, would be changed by it. It started with William Perkin's discovery of dyes that could stain cells (see chapter 2). Paul Ehrlich and his colleagues used those dyes to stain cells from patients who were considered insane. Instead, they found that they were victims of an infectious disease. Ehrlich continued his research and eventually discovered a medicine that could cure the infection and prevent the insanity. Medicine was on a steady march to defining disease with objective evidence.[5]

Unfortunately, however, most psychiatric diagnoses were still based on the personal observations of practitioners. Freud, for example, would lead the profession into a period when diagnoses were made on the basis of his scientifically unsubstantiated theories.

By 1950, psychiatry was in search of a common language that would be more objectively scientific. The search reached its goal with the publication of the Diagnostic and Statistical Manual of Mental Disorders. This book was not a text that taught the best way to treat or even diagnose the disorders included in its pages (based on a committee vote). However, it did provide an agreed-upon description of each "disease" and the criteria that had to be met to qualify for the diagnosis.

The DSM would be used to label patients with depression, anxiety, and 180 other psychiatric ailments. In 1980, the term bipolar disorder was introduced to the DSM 3rd revision in place of manic depression. The intent was to clarify the difference between manic depression and schizophrenia. But there was more to it than just simple clarification.

---

[5] Gary Greenberg, *Manufacturing Depression: The Secret History of a Modern Disease* (New York: Simon & Schuster, 2010), 56–57.

At the same time, the committee also introduced new classifications of bipolar disorder II, cyclothymia, and bipolar disorder NOS (not otherwise specified). Before this change was made, a patient had to be hospitalized with a life-disrupting episode of mania to receive a diagnosis of manic depression (now referred to as bipolar disorder I). Now, much less demanding criteria allowed physicians and psychologists considerable latitude in making the diagnosis. This soon led to increased diagnoses of the disorder.

Identifying the Categories of Bipolar Disorder

The difference between bipolar disorder I and bipolar disorder II centers on mania. Millions of people today have been diagnosed with bipolar disorder—perhaps as many as 15 million when you include all the variations. But when you only look at bipolar disorder I (the old manic depression), the number might be as small as half a million. The difference in the two groups is important, particularly when it comes to medical treatment. To clearly understand that difference, it will be helpful to look at a couple of composite cases.

Tom and Bipolar Disorder I

My first visit with Tom took place because he had been placed on medical leave by his company. He was a thirty-year-old who was sent home one day because he had nearly become involved in a fight with fellow employees over events taking place in the Middle East. At that time Tom was convinced that Jesus was coming again and that he was receiving messages from his television about it. He believed he had an important mission to accomplish that only he could carry out. In short, he was psychotic.

Psychosis is a state in which people believe things that are not true and see and hear things that no one else does. Their speech may be incoherent and they may be agitated. They are unaware that those around them do not understand their behavior or thoughts. They are unable to distinguish real things from imagined ones. It is as if they are acting in a movie that no one else can see or hear.

Their disconnection with reality often keeps them from carrying out the normal activities of daily living.

Tom talked incessantly about his mission (and many other things) in a distracted manner. He had not slept more than two or three hours a night for over a week and did not seem rational in thought or speech. He had been taken directly from his office to a local emergency room. The physician had prescribed a medication commonly used to treat the psychosis associated with bipolar disorder.

At the time of our first visit, he was sleeping well again and seemed to understand that the messages from his television were not real. This was not the first time such things had happened to Tom. He'd had at least two other experiences like this in the previous ten years. In those episodes, he had gone on financially ruinous, impulsive spending sprees. In the years between the episodes, he led a fairly routine life with some intervals of insomnia and extra energy. He had lost two jobs, one after each episode. He also had periods of depression after the episodes of mania. On both occasions, he was treated with medications that he eventually stopped due to their side effects and expense.

Tom is an example of what the DSM defines as bipolar disorder I, formerly called manic depression.[6] Tom had a one-week period of abnormally irritable, elevated, or expansive mood. His concern over his mission seemed to make him irritable. He also had an inflated sense of self-worth and a decreased need for sleep. He was very talkative and easily distracted. He also was intent on meeting the goal of his mission. Unlike some with bipolar disorder I, Tom had not been on any spending sprees, made any foolish business decisions, or involved himself in any sexual indiscretions during this episode. But his similarity to the salesman I observed in the 1970s was obvious.

Psychosis Made Tom's Problem Distinctive

The things that made Tom's problem distinctive were his psychosis, paranoia, and combativeness. First, he was hearing voices telling

---

[6] *Diagnostic and Statistical Manual of Mental Disorders*, 362.

him things that no one else heard or knew to be true. Second, his paranoia was seen in his belief that people at work were out to get him, which led to the near fistfight there. These problems separate his experience from the other 90 percent of people labeled bipolar each year. The fight nearly cost him his job, made him unable to work for a time, and almost required psychiatric hospitalization. Had Tom lacked good support at home, or had his behavior been more bizarre, he would have been admitted to the hospital. Since Tom has no other medical problem to explain his behavior and no history of substance abuse, he qualified for the diagnosis of bipolar disorder I.

Eventually Tom's mania passed and he struggled with a sense of depression. He stayed in a depressed mood with no interest in the things he had enjoyed before the mania. This mood was noticed by his friends and family. He avoided social gatherings. He had been an avid runner, but no longer ran. Because of his lack of exercise, he began to gain weight. He dropped out of church and stopped reading his Bible. He struggled with sleep unless he took his medicine.

Tom did not seem to have the energy to do his work. The problems his mania had caused at work left him feeling worthless and guilt-ridden. He had difficulty thinking and at times he wondered

---

The *Diagnostic Statistical Manual of Mental Disorders* divides Bipolar Disorder into the following categories:

- Bipolar I includes both mania and major depression.
- Bipolar II includes both major depression and hypomania.
- Another category is major depression and no mania—some blood relatives have had mania.
- A hypomanic episode includes behavior that is similar to, but less intense than, mania.
- In a mixed episode, the patient will show both depression and mania daily for a week.
- A patient may have mania and no depression.
- Cyclothymia includes mild depression and hypomania.[7]

---

[7] *Diagnostic and Statistical Manual of Mental Disorders,* Text Revision, Fourth Edition (Copyright 2000). American Psychiatric Association, 382-404.

if he would be better off dead. In both mania and depression, there are no diagnostic physical or laboratory findings to make the diagnosis clear-cut. The diagnosis is made solely on the basis of behavior, though in a case like this, the behaviors are relatively uncommon and very distinct. This form of bipolar disorder is distinct from bipolar disorder II.

Susan and Hypomania

Susan and the young single mother I met shared the label of bipolar disorder II. Both of them would have simply said that they were "bipolar" along with millions of others today. None of the doctors thought it important to tell them the difference between bipolar I and II because they doubted they would understand the distinction. While their stories were different from Tom's, the issue all three had in common was depression.

The young mother and Susan worked their way through a number of antidepressants and "mood stabilizers" meant for the treatment of bipolar disorder. Tom was taking one of the same mood stabilizers for the treatment of bipolar disorder I. The difference between them was that Susan and the mother were not benefiting much from the medication, but Tom was. Susan struggled with the medicine and its side effects. Tom, on the other hand, did not have manic episodes or depression as long as he took his medicine.

If these three had the same ailment, they all should have benefited from medication aimed at stabilizing manic moods. This raises the same question we face with depression. If the diagnostic criteria are vague and no test can validate the diagnosis of bipolar disorder, has this led us to apply the diagnosis of bipolar disorder to people who do not actually have it?

I would say that the answer is yes, and there are others in the field who agree. David Healy[8] said the following concerning the current state of affairs for bipolar disorder: "If we consider adults alone for a moment, there is already the potential for creating an

---

[8]David Healy is professor of psychiatry and director of the North Wales Department of Psychological Medicine at Cardiff University.

'epidemic' of bipolar disorder, because people are being diagnosed with the condition based on operational criteria that depend upon subjective judgments (rather than an objective criterion of disability, such as hospitalization or being off work for a month)."[9]

What Healy is telling us is this: Before 1980, you had to have a life-disrupting episode (including mania) that resulted in your hospitalization before you could get a diagnosis of bipolar disorder I. The diagnosis was subjective, but the criteria limited the diagnosis to those most seriously affected.

Today, there are still a small number of people like Tom being clearly diagnosed with bipolar disorder I, but we also have a huge number of Susans who have received the same diagnosis, even though they have never had mania or a life-disrupting hospitalization. They received the diagnosis because a new criterion or symptom was added to the list: hypomania.

Hypomania is supposed to be the same kind of definitive diagnostic symptom for bipolar disorder II that mania is for bipolar disorder I. Mania was the critical element in the diagnosis of manic depression or bipolar I for people like the salesman and Tom. The inability to sleep for days at a time, talking a mile a minute, and suffering hallucinations and delusions of grandeur made these people easy to identify. Couple those behaviors with disastrous spending or sexual indiscretion and individuals with mania can be easily (and reliably) diagnosed. It was not difficult for Tom's wife to call me when she recognized that his problems were coming on. The behavior is distinctive and observable, and the number of people affected is relatively small.

But bipolar disorder II is a different matter. The criteria for bipolar disorder II include the following:

A. Presence (or history) of one or more major depressive episodes.

B. Presence (or history) of at least one hypomanic episode.

---

[9]David Healy, "The Latest Mania: Selling Bipolar Disorder," PLoS Medicine3 (4): e185, April 11, 2006, 6. Electronically retrieved on 3–28–2012.

C. There never has been a manic episode or a mixed episode (of depression and mania).

D. The mood symptoms in criteria A and B are not better accounted for by schizoaffective disorder and are not super-imposed on schizophrenia, schizophreniform disorder, delusional disorder, or psychotic disorder not otherwise specified.

E. The symptoms cause significant clinical distress or impairment in social, occupational, or other important areas of functioning.[10]

To qualify for the diagnosis of bipolar disorder II, an individual must have both a major depression episode and a hypomanic episode. Hypomania has its own set of criteria. In essence it is a period of time that looks something like mania but does not meet the criteria for it.

The criteria for hypomania are on the following page.[11]

The significant differences between Tom's easily recognized mania and the newer bipolar II diagnosis are found in the duration of the problem and the presence or absence of psychosis, delusions, or hallucinations. To qualify as having hypomania, you only need to meet the criteria for four days. A diagnosis of mania requires at least a week's worth of problems—and they are big problems. They involve more than lacking energy to get your work done or being a bit more talkative.

The main difference is that hypomania does not have to cause impairment. In some cases, hypomania may look like an improvement and not a symptom of a disease because the patient may seem more energetic, talkative, and even happy. Unlike mania, which can result in a hospitalization or the loss of your job or family, it is much less difficult to meet the criteria for hypomania. That might have been a good thing had there been a way to scientifically confirm

---

[10]*Diagnostic and Statistical Manual,* 397.
[11]*Diagnostic and Statistical Manual of Mental Disorders,* Text Revision, Fourth Edition (Copyright 2000). *American Psychiatric Association,* 368.

Criteria for Hypomanic Episode

A. A distinct period of persistently elevated, expansive, or irritable mood, lasting at least 4 days, that is clearly different from the usual non-depressed mood

B. During the period of mood disturbance, three (or more) of the following symptoms have persisted (four if the mood is only irritable) and have been present to a significant degree:

(1) Inflated self-esteem or grandiosity

(2) Decreased need for sleep (e. g., feels rested after only three hours of sleep)

(3) More talkative than usual or feels pressure to keep talking

(4) Flight of ideas or subjective experience that thoughts are racing

(5) Distractibility (i. e., attention too easily drawn to unimportant or irrelevant external stimuli)

(6) Increase in goal-directed activity (socially, at work or school, or sexually) or psychomotor agitation

(7) Excessive involvement in pleasurable activities that have a high potential for painful consequences (e. g., unrestrained buying sprees, sexual indiscretions, or foolish business investments)

C. The episode is associated with an unequivocal change in functioning that is uncharacteristic of the person when not symptomatic.

D. The disturbance in mood and the change in functioning are observable by others.

E. The episode (1) is not severe enough to cause marked impairment in social or occupational functioning, (2) does not necessitate hospitalization, and (3) does not have psychotic features.

F. The symptoms are not due to the direct physiological effects of a substance (e. g., a drug of abuse, a medication, or other treatment) or a general medical condition (e. g., hyperthyroidism).

Note: Hypomanic-like episodes that are clearly caused by somatic antidepressant treatment (e. g., medication, ECT, light therapy) should not count toward a diagnosis of bipolar II disorder.

the diagnosis of bipolar disorder II and hypomania, but there is not. As a result, bipolar disorder II faces the same problems with validity that we saw earlier with depression.

The result of the broadened, lower standard for this diagnosis is that people like Susan are caught in the diagnosis. They have struggled with a depressed mood without much improvement on antidepressant medication, and are reclassified as having bipolar disorder because they report symptoms like those listed in the DSM. But there is a catch to it.

The catch for Susan and many more Americans is this cautionary statement in the DSM-IV criteria for hypomania: "Hypomanic episodes . . . are clearly caused by somatic antidepressant treatment. . . . "[12] That is, medicine prescribed for depression can cause the kinds of behaviors and symptoms that are considered primary symptoms of bipolar disorder II. It may be that our treatment of depression with current antidepressants is the cause of many of the symptoms that lead to a diagnosis of bipolar disorder II.

Instead of treating a new disease, we may simply be treating the side effects of a drug used to treat an old one. And that brings us back to depression and what to do about bipolar disorder. This chapter began with the premise that we are overdiagnosing depression today in people who are simply sad over losing something they sincerely believed they could not live without. The solution is the same as it always has been in medicine. We need to make a better diagnosis based on the most solid factual evidence we can get. Then we should help people with medication or counseling that has been shown to be effective without intolerable side effects.

---

[12] *Diagnostic and Statistical Manual of Mental Disorders*, 36.

15

Helping Those with Bipolar Disorder

If we are going to help people with depressed moods and those labeled bipolar, the most important thing we can do is to clarify the difference between bipolar disorder I and bipolar disorder II. While the diagnosis of bipolar disorder II is nebulous, bipolar disorder I is not. That is the place to start. This is important to those who counsel individuals with this diagnosis, particularly those who counsel people from the Bible.

Tom needs his medicine. He also needs a compelling reason to take it. If Tom does not take his medicine, in a few days he won't be sleeping. He will be making plans regarding his work future or his finances that others will call grandiose. Tom's friends and I have an agreement that, when he seems headed in the direction of mania, they call me and we manage the dose of his medication to meet his need. Because of this, it has been years since Tom has had a significant episode of mania.

The result is that Tom has been able to keep his job and support his family. A while back, Tom came to see me while he was on the verge of a manic episode. He really wanted to stop taking the medication that seemed to help him avoid mania. I thought about it a moment and then asked him who would support his family when he lost his job. There sat Tom, a fine Christian man, a husband with several small children. And even with his mind racing a little, Tom knew what he had to do. He took his medicine.

It is vitally important for individuals who have had multiple episodes of mania to continue their medication if they wish to avoid the grief that usually comes from stopping it. I believe it was my job, as a physician who counsels people like Tom from the Bible, to emphasize the importance of being able to function as the head of his household, the best husband he could be for his wife, and the best father he could be for his children. This meant he needed to keep his job. Tom understood and took his medicine despite the side effects he did not like. I will always admire him for that.

There are many other issues that Tom needed to deal with in counseling that go beyond the scope of this book. It is safe to say that when Tom is not manic, he has the same kinds of problems we all face. Anger, worry, finances, parenting, work, and being a good husband were things he dealt with like the rest of us. Tom would need counseling that guided him to biblical solutions for all of these problems. The Scriptures are sufficient in all matters of life and godliness and we should be prepared to offer biblical answers to these problems even when counseling people who are labeled bipolar.[1] The promise applies to them too.

Who Is Responsible?

I wrote this book because I have been questioned frequently by counselors who are seeing more people with the label bipolar. Some of those so labeled have said they were not responsible for their behavior and could not change it because they had bipolar disorder. The counselors wanted to know if these individuals were responsible for sin they committed during an episode of mania. In other words, did bipolar disorder cause them to sin?

A good answer to that question came in a lecture given by Dr. Ed Welch at the Christian Counseling Education Foundation (CCEF)

---

[1] 2 Peter 1:3.

conference in Louisville, Kentucky in the fall of 2011.[2] He had counseled a man who struggled with bipolar disorder I (the old manic depression). During an episode of mania ten years earlier, he had committed adultery and his wife separated from him as a result. Now the man and his wife were considering reconciliation and came in to discuss it.

At the beginning of the session, the man said he believed that the sin he committed earlier was due to the mania of his bipolar disorder. Dr. Welch replied that the Scriptures tell us that our sin comes out of our own hearts and that mania could not cause him to sin.[3] In time, the man accepted this and eventually the couple reconciled. A short time later he had another manic episode, but this time the outcome was different. Brothers in Christ kept track of the man as he made his way through the episode of mania. This time he did not commit adultery.

While bipolar mania[4] may place a person at greater risk of making a bad choice in life, it does not decide if he will choose to sin or not. Tom faced the same kind of choice when he was on the edge of mania. In light of what I told him, he made a choice that benefited his family. My experience leads me to believe that those with bipolar disorder I are not irresistibly compelled to sin because of the diagnosis. They do need brothers and sisters in Christ who are willing to stay close to them when they start to struggle. Like all of us, they need someone to hold them accountable, love them, pray for them, and walk with them when their minds race towards problem behavior.

Among the patients I have cared for and counseled with the mania of bipolar I, those who have been willing to follow the counsel of Scripture and follow their medical care plan have generally done well during manic episodes. It has also been my experience that people who have only had one episode of mania (or anything

---

[2]Dr. Ed Welch, "What You Can Do to Help," General Session 4 at Christian Counselling and Educational Foundation conference, October, 2011. Approximately 28 minutes into the lecture.
[3]See James 1:14–22 and 4:1–10.
[4]The mania in both cases did not include psychosis. Psychosis is different in that the patient may not know at the time who he is, where he is, or what he is doing and may require hospitalization.

like it) will want to stop their medication at some point to see if they really need it.

I have had more than one patient tell me that they had been identified as having bipolar I mania but never had it again after the first episode. They argue persuasively against taking medicine for twenty years to avoid something that did not happen again. And I cannot disagree with them. I have also seen individuals who had multiple episodes of mania because they stopped their medicine—and I have seen the life-wrenching problems that generally go with this decision.

No one who reads this should ever stop taking his medicine or change his dose without talking with the physician who prescribed it. At the same time, it would not be unreasonable for a person who has only had one episode of mania to talk with his or her physician about stopping the medicine after six months to a year, while under close supervision by friends and family. Those, like Tom, who have had multiple episodes of mania are probably best served by continuing to take their medicine.

Bipolar II and Hypomania

The most important observation I have made in dealing with people who carry the bipolar label is the difference between the Toms and the Susans. Bipolar disorder II, if medically untreated, does not have the same outcome as bipolar disorder I with mania. There is no good medical explanation for the rise in the number of people diagnosed with bipolar disorder II, except for the fact that it did not exist as a diagnosis in the DSM until 1980. However, as noted earlier, the criteria do give us another hint.

The cautionary note at the end of the description of hypomania says that medication used to treat depression may cause the symptoms that are used to make the diagnosis of bipolar disorder. It is safe to say that a significant number of people who have been diagnosed with bipolar disorder II were first diagnosed with depression and treated with an antidepressant.[5]

---

[5]David Healy, "The Latest Mania." Eli Lilly used the scenario of a patient whose physician never saw her in hypomania but only in depression. As a result the patient was treated with

Instead of seeing a rapid increase in a new disease, we may simply be seeing a rapid increase in patients diagnosed with depression who have side effects from medication that look like hypomania. Starting in 1980, the then new DSM-3 criteria led to an explosion in the diagnosis of depression. In 1984, studies showed that depression existed in anywhere from 3 to 6 percent of our population. By 2005 a study raised that number to 20 percent of the population and in 2009 another study said that depression affected up to 40 percent of our population.[6]

This diagnostic explosion has led to a similar explosion in treatment with antidepressant medications. From 1995 to 2005, the use of antidepressant medication has doubled.[7] It is reasonable to say that the change in the way we diagnose depression and the medicines we use to treat it are the source of the growing numbers of people being diagnosed with bipolar disorder II. And that brings us to the question of what we can do to address the dual diagnostic explosion of depression and bipolar disorder II.

As noted in chapter 5, Horwitz and Wakefield make a good case for the idea that 90 percent of depression in the United States is really sadness over loss. If we want to help people being swept up by the rising tide of depression and bipolar disorder diagnoses, the place to start is to challenge the misidentification of sadness as depression. Bipolar disorder I (the old manic depression) has always been with us and likely always will be. People affected by it need medical treatment—as well as counseling to help them deal with the kinds of problems we all face.

Those with bipolar disorder II should be helped as we would help anyone who is sad and struggling with loss in life. If we deal with sadness over loss as an emotion God created in us to lead us in his direction, perhaps we can return to the rates of depression we saw in this country before 1950. At the same time, maybe we

---

a standard antidepressant such as Lilly's Prozac.

[6]Alan Horwitz, "Creating an Age of Depression: The Social Construction and Consequences of the Major Depression Diagnosis," *Society and Mental Health*, the publication of the American Sociological Association, 2011:1:41, 48.

[7]Sharon Begley, "Antidepressants Don't Work/Do Work: The Debate Over the Nation's Most Popular Pills," *Newsweek*, February 8, 2010, p. 35.

as a people can regain the certainty that whatever God allows into our lives will be for our good and his glory.

Doing nothing about a depressed mood or sadness is not a solution. Denying that it exists does not help either. Instead we should be facing sadness and our losses in life in the light of Scripture. When we do that, we can grow and become more like Christ. We also have the privilege of comforting others with the comfort he gives us.[8]

If it is true that nearly 90 percent of depression today is really loss-induced sadness and that "talk therapy" (psychotherapy emphasizing conversation between therapist and patient) is just as effective as medication, then biblical counseling is in a unique position to help.[9] We have churches full of people who can be trained to speak the truth of God's Word in love to people who are struggling with loss. As the psalmist said, "The law of the LORD is perfect, restoring the soul; The testimony of the LORD is sure, making wise the simple. The precepts of the LORD are right, rejoicing the heart; The commandment of the LORD is pure, enlightening the eyes" (Ps. 19:7–9). And we get to share that Word with anyone who wants to listen, and witness the fruit born in that person's life by the power of the Spirit of God. We should not consign people to the broken cisterns of questionable diagnoses and cures when we can offer them the living water of God. May God equip, empower and move us to share that hope with others.

---

[8] 2 Corinthians 1:3–4.
[9] Sharon Begley, p. 39.

Appendix A: Finding Peace in a Person

Several times in this book I have talked about the gracious relationship we can have with God through his son Jesus. Understanding the nature of that relationship makes all the difference in dealing with the stresses and strains of life. The best way I know to explain how you can have that relationship for yourself is to tell you my story.

I did not grow up in an entirely Christian home. My parents were good people who became Christians when I was about twelve. After that, we went to church on Wednesdays and Sundays and I regularly heard the gospel. I remember being interviewed by the pastor of our church when our family sought to become members. This required us to be baptized again by immersion, though most of us had been sprinkled as children.

I remember asking my dad what I was supposed to say to the pastor when he asked me about my relationship with Christ. My father correctly told me that if the pastor asked me if I was Christian, I should answer that I was, "by grace and through faith." The pastor did ask me that question and I responded just like Dad told me. The pastor seemed satisfied and, for the second time in my life, I was baptized and a member of a church.

It seemed simple enough, but there was one problem with it all. While most everyone else in my family had truly trusted in the death and resurrection of Christ for their salvation, I just said that I did. What followed, from the time I was thirteen until I was nineteen, was a quiet, methodical rebellion against the restrictions placed on me, which seemed to come from my parents' growing faith. I worked to look the part of the fine, upstanding, young Christian, but I was not. What did I really want to do? All the things my friends at school did that got them into trouble.

In my heart I knew my parents were right, but I just wanted to be like everyone else. I did not want stand out in the crowd as a shining example of faith in action. I couldn't have done it anyway—because I did not have any faith. At the same time, I really did want to be a doctor. I had made that decision when I was eleven years old. When it was time to go to college, my parents decided that I could stay home and attend the commuter campus of Indiana University. I think they knew that my religion was simply skin deep and they doubted that I could spiritually survive campus life.

College Crisis

It was in that first year that God began to graciously work in my life in a way I could not ignore. My first year in college was a major adjustment. For the first time in my life, I really had to work to get things done. My grades that year simply would not have gotten me into medical school; in fact, it looked very much like I could fail. I began a curious process of making deals with God over medical school.

I decided that the reason I was struggling in calculus was tied to my lack of interest in anything Christian. I did not exactly pray the prayer, "Oh God, get me into medical school and I will change." Instead, I just started to do the things I thought would make God happy enough to bless my academic mess. I started reading my Bible, paying attention in church, praying (usually about coming tests), and teaching Sunday school. I did everything my church said I ought to do. And, just like the rich young ruler who told Jesus that he had kept all the commandments from his youth, I was still clueless. I was thoroughly lost.

In the process, I became an even better hypocrite than I had been before. I wasn't doing any of these good things to glorify and honor God. I wasn't teaching Sunday school for the benefit of the fourth grade boys! I was earning points aimed at raising my grade point average through divine intervention. I was worried, obsessed with school, and, despite all of my effort, I had no peace. There was nothing to enjoy about any of the things I was doing in school, church, work, or home. I was becoming my greatest fear, a failure who felt miserable.

There was one redeeming element in all the things I was doing. I was reading my Bible—three chapters a day and four on Sunday because that was what my pastor said I had to do to finish in a year. At the beginning, it was simply part of the legalism I was creating for myself, but it did not stay that way. It is a dangerous thing to read the Bible daily and ask God for help—unless you really want it.

A Provocative Question

I remember the day I realized that I did not have a good reason to read my Bible or do the rest of the religious things I was doing. It was also the day I began to understand that I was no more a Christian than someone who lived in the Amazon jungle and had never heard of Jesus. I owe that to Mrs. Seldon, my first history professor.

Mrs. Seldon was the first person to challenge any part of my faith in college. She didn't mean to; for all I know, she may have been a believer and may have meant to say that the word "trinity" did not appear in the Bible. But one day she told our class that the Trinity never appears in the Bible. At the end of class, I walked up to her desk and started showing her passages of Scripture that substantiated the existence of the Trinity as God in three persons: God the Father, Son, and Holy Spirit.

She was very gracious and found it all very interesting. At the end of our conversation, she asked a question that would change my life. "Why do you read the Bible?" she asked. I don't believe she was being antagonistic in any way; I think she really wondered why. I was dumbfounded. I stumbled around for an answer and said something like, "It's good for me." She had asked me a question just like Jesus had asked that rich young ruler. "Why do you call me good?" "Why do you read this Bible?"

Finding the Answer

From that point on, I began to look for the answer. I found it or, rather, I found him. One night, sitting in my parents' dining room, I was reading in John's gospel. I got to chapter 14 and read Jesus' words to his disciples before their walk to the garden of Gethsemane, the trial, and the cross. For the first time in my life, I saw Jesus and, as I read the words, it was just like Jesus was there talking to me.

> "Do not let your heart be troubled; believe in God, believe also in Me. In My Father's house are many dwelling places; if it were not so, I would have told you; for I go to prepare a place for you. If I go and prepare a place for you, I will come again and receive you to Myself, that where I am, there you may be also. And you know the way where I am going." Thomas said to Him, "Lord, we do not know where You are going, how do we know the way?" Jesus said to him, "I am the way, and the truth, and the life; no one comes to the Father but through Me."
>
> —John 14:1–6

There Jesus was telling me what I needed most. My heart was troubled; I was struggling to make myself a better person so God would approve. Instead, Jesus was telling me to believe in him. He also told me that if I would abide in him, my life would be fruitful and useful. He also prayed for me. "I do not ask on behalf of these alone, but for those also who believe in Me through their word" (John 17:20).

By then, my reading had taken me lots of places in the Bible and it told me about grace. "For by grace you have been saved through faith; and that not of yourselves, it is the gift of God; not as a result of works, so that no one may boast. For we are His workmanship, created in Christ Jesus for good works, which God prepared beforehand so that we would walk in them" (Eph. 2:8–10). These verses were the source of the answer my dad had told me to tell my pastor years before. Now I understood them.

All my good works could never solve my real problem. I was, as all men are, a sinner, and I had miserably fallen short of God's glory (Rom. 3:23). Nothing in the world I could do would change that.

Receiving the Gift

But God's grace could. He providentially sent a history professor to tell me what I knew deep in my heart. I was a lost sinner needing God's grace if I was ever going to be saved. I repented of my effort to save myself by my good works. I had to receive the gift of eternal life just like everyone else.

Later, on my way home from work at a stoplight at two in the morning, I bowed my head and told God that I was a hopeless sinner and I believed that Jesus had died for me so that he could give me eternal life. Paul said, "Whoever will call on the name of the Lord will be saved," and I believed it. Since that day, I have never doubted that God saved me by his grace (Rom. 10:13). For the first time in my life, I had peace and eternal life.

It has been four decades since that evening. Since then, God has enabled me to deal with worry and loss by his grace. To the reader who has come this far in search of freedom from worry and bad moods, I encourage you to do the same thing I did. Join the rest of us who have abandoned trying to fix a broken life on our own. Instead, change your mind and believe on the name of Jesus Christ so that you can have the gift of eternal life and the peace that comes with it.

Jesus put it best when he said, "Come to Me, all who are weary and heavy-laden, and I will give you rest. Take My yoke upon you and learn from Me, for I am gentle and humble in heart, and YOU WILL FIND REST FOR YOUR SOULS. For My yoke is easy and My burden is light" (Matt. 11:28–30). The choice is to keep carrying the heavy burden of worry and sadness or to put it down and follow Christ. I hope you choose Christ.

Appendix B: Diseases That Affect Mood

This book has talked extensively about the reasons why diagnoses of depression often do not reflect an accurate understanding of a person's problem. We have seen that these diagnoses are typically made when a medical professional makes a subjective assessment of the patient's behavior, based on criteria specified in the *Diagnostic and Statistical Manual of Mental Disorders.* If a person demonstrates enough of the DSM criteria for two weeks or more, many medical professionals will say that the person has a disease and will prescribe medication to treat it. This book has argued that, in many cases, some symptoms of depression and bipolar disorder that are observed may actually be side effects of the medications prescribed to relieve the problem.

Having said that, however, I also want to acknowledge that there are times when a depressed mood *is* a symptom of a physical disease and *does* require medication. This reality is very important for those who counsel and care for people with mood and medical problems.

When individuals come to my office with a depressed mood, I ask them when they last saw their primary physician. If they have not seen their doctor for a year or more, I send them back to their doctor for a thorough physical and appropriate laboratory tests and imaging. I do that because sometimes the behavior that prompts people to seek counseling may be tied to an underlying medical problem that can be corrected with medical care.

There are many diseases that can alter mood and behavior. One example is pica, a behavior that sometimes accompanies anemia. Anemia due to a lack or loss of iron is not an uncommon medical problem, but pica is very unusual. With pica, when a patient's iron level drops below normal, children and adults are known to eat items that are not food. Children eat dirt and wall board and both adults and children eat ice. When the anemia is treated and iron levels return to normal, the behavior stops. Sometimes simply starting oral iron supplements will end the desire to eat ice.

If you did not know that the child or adult was anemic, this unusual behavior could be interpreted in lots of ways. Parents might think that their child was disobedient and defiant if the child kept eating dirt after they told him to stop. Adults who eat whole bags of carrots or gallons of ice cream (other behaviors associated with pica) might be considered strange. Their dentists might be glad to put crowns on teeth that are cracked by crunching on ice, but they might wonder why someone would do it again and again. But when a doctor orders a complete blood panel, the iron deficiency is discovered and the behavior becomes understandable—and treatable.

As a physician, I know that my profession has been notorious at times for assigning psychological causes to behavior that really had a physiological origin. That was why Paul Ehrlich's use of purple dye to stain and study tissue and identify correctible physical diseases in mental patients was so significant. If there is a physical problem that can be cured with medication, we want our patients to have it. I do not want to be counseling someone for anxiety when he or she should be treated for hyperthyroidism. That is why I send my counselees back to see their doctor. That way I won't be advising parents on how to gain control of their child's rebellious dirt-eating behavior when the child really needs some iron!

It is beyond the scope of this book to survey all the physical diseases known to have mood and behavioral changes associated with them. A better approach might be to look at the categories of diseases and discuss a few of them. However, please note: Nothing in this appendix can take the place of a thorough examination by a trusted physician. If the information given here spurs you to send people who struggle with their moods to see their doctor, it will be worthwhile.[1]

Metabolic and Endocrine Disease

There are at least a dozen diseases in this category that are accompanied at times by a depressed mood. They include abnormalities like the following:

1. *Hyper and hypothyroidism.* Thyroids that put out too much or too little hormone have an effect on the way our brains function. The thyroid controls our metabolic rate. Abnormalities in either direction can result in a depressed or an anxious mood.

2. *Hyperparathyroidism* and the resultant elevated serum calcium can lead to a depressed mood, lethargy, and psychosis.

3. *Low serum potassium* or *hypokalemia*, and *low serum sodium* or *hyponatremia* are both associated with mood disturbances.

4. *Cushing's disease* is caused by an excess of glucocortoids (steroid-like substances) that are caused by pituitary tumors, adrenal gland tumors and prescription medication such as prednisone. Affected patients may experience agitated depression, mood swings, irritability, anxiety, panic attacks and paranoia.

5. *Addison's disease* is caused by a lack of adrenal gland output of substances similar to the glucocortoids of Cushing's disease. This is a serious problem that can present with depression and psychosis.

6. *Hypopituitarism* is a condition in which the pituitary gland fails to make and secrete hormones that control the thyroid, adrenal glands, and other endocrine glands. When it fails to function, the thyroid and other endocrine glands also fail to function. This condition can be associated with a depressed mood.

7. *Porphyria* is an inherited disease related to hemoglobin production. It results in neurologic damage to many body systems

---

[1]Source material for this appendix comes from Uptodate.com, an internet service that provides current information on a wide variety of medical subjects. Electronically retrieved at uptodate.com 4/16/2012.

and can cause significant abdominal pain and neurologic disorders. Patients may experience depression, psychosis, delirium, anxiety, disorientation, hysteria and altered consciousness.

8. *Wilson's disease* is a disorder related to copper metabolism and *Wernicke-Korsakoff's* disease is the result of a dietary lack of thiamine often seen in chronic alcohol abuse. Both diseases can result in mood problems and a decline in mental function.

Infections and Depression

Infectious disease is also associated with depression. Diseases such as tuberculosis, mononucleosis, HIV, encephalitis, influenza, pneumonia and tertiary syphilis are known to be associated with changes in brain function. Depression can be seen with any of these infections.

Neurologic Diseases

There are many diseases of the brain and nervous system that can have depression as one of the symptoms. Degenerative diseases such as Alzheimer's disease and Huntington's disease are often accompanied by depression, though it may be difficult to determine whether the depression is a symptom of the disease itself or the patient's response to contracting the disease. Multiple Sclerosis and Parkinson's disease may also be accompanied by depression.

Problems such as brain tumors, strokes, and closed head injuries may also bring a depressed mood. Subdural hematomas and normal pressure hydrocephalus can as well. Anything that causes substantial damage to brain tissue and function may be accompanied by a depressed mood.

General Problems

Cancer of any kind may be accompanied by depression. It is worth remembering that cancer of the pancreas may first present as a depressed mood. Other systemic diseases such as lupus and similar auto-immune disorders may be accompanied by depression. Congestive heart failure is known to be associated with depression as well.

Another important cause of a depressed mood is often over-looked. Sleep deprivation or sleep disturbance (for whatever reason) is a likely cause for a depressed mood in those affected. This is an important consideration in counseling. Counselees who are not sleeping at least eight hours a night should be encouraged to do so. Those who say they cannot should be sent to their physician for care.

Medication and Drugs—Legal and Otherwise

A wide variety of medications and drugs, both legal and illegal, can cause depression. The following are known to be associated with a depressed mood:

Alcohol, amphetamines, barbiturates, beta blockers, chemotherapy drugs, cholinesterase inhibitors, cimetidine (Tagamet), cocaine withdrawal, heavy metal poisoning, opiates, and steroids.

This list is far from complete. As I practice medicine these days, my first question when a patient comes with a new problem is not what new disease he has. Now I wonder what side effects he is having and which drug is causing it.

The purpose of this appendix is not to equip counselors to make medical diagnoses. But as we try to help people with mood problems, we should be aware that some depressed moods are indicators of serious physical illnesses that require medical intervention. I have not provided an exhaustive list of medical problems associated with a depressed mood, but I hope that this summary is sufficient to illustrate why no depressed person should fail to see a physician for a thorough workup and possible medical treatment.